START OF PLAY

START OF PLAY

THE CURIOUS ORIGINS OF OUR
FAVOURITE SPORTS

JONATHAN RICE

First published in 1998 in Great Britain by
Prion Books Limited
32-34 Gordon House Road,
London NW5 1LP

Copyright © Jonathan Rice 1998

ISBN 1-85375-281-9

Cover design by Bob Eames
Cover images: The Vintage Magazine Co.

Printed and bound in Great Britain
by Creative Print & Design, Wales

PICTURE ACKNOWLEDGEMENTS
Hulton Getty Picture Library 215;
Mary Evans Picture Library 19, 36, 40, 48, 55, 111, 116,
119, 127, 138, 144, 148, 164, 170, 184, 190, 196, 204
The Vintage Magazine Co. 3, 75, 128, 135, 173, 192

CONTENTS

"FOOLISH GAMES WHICH ARE NO USE"

Who invented the ball? How did the simple little globe develop into the gamut of balls that exist today – large, small, round, oval, hard, soft, leather, plastic, wood and rubber, red, black and white? How did a simple game of catch grow into the over eight hundred different ball games now played more or less regularly somewhere in the world? How do we explain Alan Ball, the English World Cup-winning midfielder, or John Ball, the amateur golfer who found his home course, Hoylake, so easy that he would play it backwards or even left-handed to keep his interest up? Why is golf so difficult to play left-handed anyway? Why is football eleven a side, rugby union fifteen a side, baseball nine a side and rugby league thirteen a side? How did all these games come about? There are two different theories to explain the origin of this species: one is mythical and the other is evolutionary.

Who invented the ball? God did, I suppose, as the globe shape exists in nature in many different natural guises. There are all sizes of round fruits, from the apple that Eve gave to Adam in the Garden of Eden, to currants and grapes, oranges, grapefruits and even watermelons and pumpkins. There are pebbles, rocks and boulders, and even knuckle bones and human skulls which are often round enough to have served as balls. Some would say that the ball has no known practical use, or at least had none until the invention of the ball-bearing, but whether the ancients actually used balls for anything other than recreation is irrelevant: the main purpose of all balls, whether big or small, round or oval, has been to play with – to throw, to catch, to hit, to kick and to run with. The ball has always been a sporting implement.

Who invented the ball? If it wasn't God, then Homer had an alternative theory. The blind Greek epic poet wrote *The Odyssey* around 900 BC about events which may have happened around three hundred years before that, so he wasn't actually there to witness the momentous sporting occasion he writes about, but that does not make him unique among journalists. He tells us unequivocally that the ball was invented by the inhabitants of Lydia, and that a woman called Anagalla of Corcyra was the first person to make a ball to play with. So that's who invented the ball. Homer goes on to tell us that when Odysseus was shipwrecked during his ten years' wandering, trying to get back home to Ithaca from the Trojan Wars, he found the Princess Nausicaa, daughter of King Alcinous of the Phaeacians, playing ball with her handmaidens by the shore. We have no idea what game she was playing, but we can assume it was some sort of bowls or skittles. This is the first recorded mention of a ball game in literature – and it was played by women, not men.

However, the unfortunate truth is that not only is the existence of Homer unproven, to say nothing of his place of birth, his date of birth and whether he (or she?) actually wrote what is now known as *The Odyssey*; also we have no absolute proof of the story of the fall of Troy, or of the subsequent wanderings of

Beware of Greeks bearing balls — the Hellenic world may have been the first to fashion a ball used for sport, but it was Victorian invention and industry that turned ball and sporting equipment manufacture into high commerce

Odysseus. We also have no idea how mythical or real the Princess Nausicaa actually was, so we have reluctantly to conclude that Homer's explanation of the invention of the ball may well be no more reliable than many back-page sports stories today. So, if Homer is not to be believed, how did the ball come into existence? Was there a moment when the idea of tossing a round object up in the air and catching it again, just for the fun of it, occurred to a bored caveman? Perhaps, on a balmy late summer evening, he was sitting like Isaac Newton under an apple tree, when a fruit fell into his hand and such was his joy at this proof of nature's bounty that he threw it up into the air. Having done this, he realised that if he was to eat it, he would need to catch the apple before it hit the ground (I am confident that the principles of gravity were known well before the laws were propounded, just as the principles of football, golf and cricket were known before the rules of those games were codified). So our caveman caught the apple, and realised that the throwing and catching was almost as much fun as eating the apple. That's as plausible an explanation as any other, and there is one thing that we can be certain of: the ball was not invented by just one person. Every ancient civilisation as far back as records go has references to balls and games played with them. Most of these games are a variation on either football or skittles, but all seem to have been purely for recreational or ceremonial purposes.

The earliest sports did not involve balls. Sport grew out of the hunter's skills, allowing those who could run quickest, throw the farthest and lift the heaviest weights to show off their skills to their peers. It was an extension of war, a means of making sure warriors had the skills needed to win battles, and hunters the skills to feed their families. Palaeolithic man, roaming around the plains of Europe up to twenty thousand years before the birth of Christ, thought that his hunting expeditions were significant enough to be recorded in cave paintings, so it seems at least very likely that these paintings were not the only way in which the hunt was celebrated. Surely there may well also have been a re-enactment of the day's work, with men proving to each other how far they really did throw their spears or how strong they really were when it came to killing their prey. These were shows of strength with no practical purpose other than to show off to one's fellows, a definition of sport which could still stand today. The best definition of sport these days is "any athletic event not performed to music". So ice dancing and gymnastics floor exercises are no more sports than are ballet or cheerleading. One can easily imagine that as soon as the bow and arrow was invented, men were challenging each other to see who could shoot an arrow the farthest or the straightest. Within minutes of the first sling being slung, men were testing their accuracy by trying to hit a rock at fifty paces; and well before any such weapons were invented, men were testing their strength in wrestling matches to discover who was the champion of the tribe. The only music involved was when songs were sung about their great champions around the campfires at night.

When Goliath of Gath challenged the Israelites three thousand years ago with the words, "Choose you a man for you, and let him come to me," he was doing so because he was "a champion out of the camp of the Philistines". A champion has to prove himself a champion, so we must assume that Goliath had done that through contests of weightlifting, throwing, wrestling or swordplay with his fellow Philistines. His supremacy was based on his size and his strength, because he was six cubits and a span tall, and he was armed with a coat of mail which weighed "five thousand shekels of brass". He was bigger and better protected than a Green Bay Packer or an ice-hockey goalminder. But David, fighting on behalf of the Israelites, disdained the armour and helmet and sword that he was offered, and just took his sling with him. He also stopped to choose "five smooth stones out of the brook", and went off to meet the mighty Goliath. Five smooth stones would fly like golf balls from the sling, although many golfers today would need to go out armed with more than five balls to do battle with that massive and uncompromising Goliath of today, their local golf course.

The story of David and Goliath tells us many things about man's attitude towards sporting competition. Firstly, professionalism rules, and it always has. In attempting to find somebody to challenge Goliath, King Saul had promised "the man who killeth him, the king will enrich him with great riches, and will give him his daughter" – a big enough payout, one would have thought, for a young shepherd boy with nothing much to lose. The second thing we learn is that if the rules are not written down before the match starts, it will not be a fair contest. The playing field will not be level, because one side or the other will look for a way to turn the circumstances to their advantage, in a way that Englishmen, almost alone among the sportsmen of the world, would describe as "not fair". All's fair in love, war and sport.

The third rule of sporting life that David v Goliath teaches us is that subtlety and timing are always better weapons than brute force. In all sports, it is the great timers of the ball, or of a stone or a fist, who are the greatest champions. Muhammad Ali, Maureen Connolly, Pelé, Michael Lynagh and Donald Bradman were probably smaller than many of their opponents, but they had the grace and the subtlety, as well as the skill, to make size unimportant.

FOOLISH GAMES WHICH ARE NO USE

Sir Flinders Petrie, the noted archaeologist and by birth and culture a typical late Victorian English gentleman, found, during his excavations on the Nile delta, implements in the grave of a child that showed that the ancient Egyptians played a game very like skittles in 5200 BC, many centuries before the completion of Homer's great work featuring Princess Nausicaa and her ball-playing handmaidens. The late John Arlott's authoritative *Oxford Companion to Sports and Games* says that "bowls probably evolved from the earliest days of history, when primitive man, in moments of relaxation, threw rocks or large stones at smaller stones or other targets".[1] A type of hockey seems to have been played in the Nile Valley around two thousand years before the birth of Christ, and different styles of football were played in places as far apart as China and the Andes over two thousand years ago. Hurling is recorded in Ireland from 1272 BC, two or three hundred years before David slew Goliath. In China a thousand years later, they played a kind of football called Tsu Chu, a game more like the modern day "keepy uppy", which also spread to Japan by the 9th century AD.

Coroibos of Olis is the first athlete whose name we know. He is also the first winner whose name has survived: he won the laurel wreath for the stadium race, a sprint of about 170 metres, in the Olympic Games of 776 BC. The Olympic Games date from the 13th century before Christ, but they did not include any ball games. In the first few Games, only foot races were held, but by the time they had flowered into the only major sporting event of the ancient world, the sports that were featured included wrestling, boxing and chariot racing. There was also a pentathlon event, covering running, wrestling, long jump, discus and javelin, but there were no ball games. The

7

ancient Olympic Games also included artistic events – poetry, music, dance and the like – to reflect the Greek ideal of the unity of physical and intellectual achievement; but no ball games.

In April 1998, archaeologists in Mexico announced that they had discovered the world's oldest court for ball games, in the south-eastern Chiapas region, at Paso de la Amada. The court dates back to around 1400 BC, two hundred years before Homer claimed Princess Nausicaa and her playmates invented the ball. The court staged contests of the mortals against the gods, and there were frequent human sacrifices involved, presumably of anybody who was on the losing side. The ball used was made of rubber, and there is evidence that the Mexicans not only played ball games but also turned them into spectator sports and opportunities for placing bets, the three key elements of professional sport today. The archaeologists who discovered the site suggest that the court, around 80 metres long and 20 metres wide, could accommodate thousands of spectators, who watched a game more like tennis than football, played by professionals who were paid by noblemen wishing to ensure favour with the gods. Similar games are still played in Mexico, one of them involving the recondite skill of keeping the ball in play without the use of either the hands or the feet, but merely by juggling the ball on the hips and buttocks. The game was certainly not football, but it was a ball game, and it was as important to the Mesoamerican Mokaya people as football's World Cup or Wimbledon or the Open golf is to us today.

One rather unlikely name on the list of potential inventors of football is Julius Caesar. When the great Roman leader was in England in 55 BC, tradition has it that he kicked a human skull across the River Brent, a tributary of the Thames, thus not only inventing a major world sport but also naming a third division football team – Brentford. However, it is possible that certain key elements of this story would not stand up to much deeper scrutiny, so on balance it would be unwise to add the invention of football to the other more provable achievements of Julius Caesar. Even his action in using a human skull as a ball was probably not original. In India they used a human head wrapped in muslin as the ball in games of polo for centuries before the arrival of the Europeans. The first description of a game of polo dates back to around 600 BC, in the works of the Persian poet Firdausi, who filed a rhyming match report of the international between the Persians and the Turkomans. We are not told how many chukkas each human head lasted for, but presumably there was quite a demand for further supplies as the game grew ever more popular. The cry of "new balls, please" must have sent shivers down the spines of the residents of the local maharajah's gaols. Not that human heads were the only raw materials for polo balls. The name "polo" derives from the word *pulu*, denoting the willow root from which the balls were more usually made.

Despite Caesar's inventive genius, for at least one thousand years after the collapse of the Greek civilisation and the end of the Olympic Games, there was, in Europe at least, little record of anything resembling organised athletic pastimes. Life was hard enough just getting through the day without having time or energy left to take part in energetic games just for fun. The official church attitude at the time was also disapproving of any such frivolity, and the only sporting activity until the later Middle Ages was in the phoney wars of jousting (for the knightly class only), archery, wrestling and hawking. People still tested their strength against each other, but there is not much evidence of social advancement for those who were mighty wrestlers or wonderful archers.

The knights, however, won extra status through their jousting skills, but very often this status was not long-lasting. Usually, the tournaments, which eventually were to provide a colourful backdrop to many Hollywood mediaeval romances, were nothing like the celluloid image of well-organised displays of knights charging at each other, lances levelled for the strike. The princess sits on the right-hand side of her uncle, the king, and prays inwardly that she will be allowed to marry the dashing but unknown horseman who has just arrived at the joust and who has bravely challenged the evil and black-helmeted Sir Grimond de Mort, even though he must make do with a broken shield and a tattered banner, while Sir Grimond has all the latest and most colourful weapons technology at his disposal. Tournaments were much more shambolic affairs than that, described by one authority as "the most exciting, expensive, ruinous and delightful activity of the noble class"[2], often lasting as long as a week or more with hundreds of knights taking part. They were the great sporting events of the day, attracting large crowds, and so were of necessity fought over a fairly small patch of land, to allow the spectators to get a reasonable view of the action. The inevitable result was that more knights died through suffocation in the crush of horses and armour in such a confined space than from a clean blow with a lance or a sword. In 1240, for example, some sixty knights were killed at a tournament near Cologne, but despite the church's outspoken disapproval, the tournaments went on. Death in a tournament was considered to be the mortal sin of suicide, but for the knights, who were professional soldiers often without a real battle to fight, the lure of danger and extreme physical activity was far stronger than the risk of excommunication or an eternity in hell.

For the crowds, the tournament was a great event, a kind of "Grand National meets Wimbledon" week, to which everybody in the area made their way. Not even the Black Death could prevent tournaments going ahead, attracting the nobility and their families and retainers as well as the local shopkeepers, tradesmen, thieves, entertainers, prostitutes and drunks. In the 13th and 14th centuries, they represented the best opportunities all classes of society had of mingling together in a common purpose, but they were nevertheless hardly truly democratic events. They were days of excitement for all who were involved, but designed to maintain the social hierarchy rather than upset it. In that, they resembled nothing so much as the Eton versus Harrow matches at Lord's in the 1870s.

Perhaps the main legacy of the tournaments to future generations of sportsmen, apart from the ability to appear civilised while actually behaving like an unprincipled thug, was in the wearing of colours. It is not true to say that colours had never been worn at sporting events before the era of the tournaments, but the use of colours by the knights, which obviously was a continuation of the wearing of colours and flying of standards on the battlefield, was a feature that has continued as a way of telling opponents apart in almost every modern sport.

Tournaments also marked the beginning of the tradition of *shamateurism*. David had been a straightforward professional when he slew Goliath, taking the fight for the money (and the promise of the hand of King Saul's daughter in marriage). But the noble knights were not motivated by the thought of material wealth or the prospect of becoming the king's son-in-law. Indeed, the feudal code of chivalry gave no thought to mone-

tary gain. But the winners at the tournaments were big financial winners, too, because the loser had to pay a ransom to the
winner, and forfeit his horse and his armour and often his servants to his conqueror. Thus, the victors became wealthy while
retaining their amateur status, and the losers often chose a quick
death to a life of penury and obligation.

For the rest of the population, the feudal system and the
harsh realities of life did not encourage selfish enjoyment in idle
sports. As the hierarchical and patriarchal systems of government slowly relaxed across Europe in the later Middle Ages,
however, ball games began to take up more and more time for
all sectors of the population, but they still almost always
brought down the full weight of official disapproval on the
heads of the participants. Ball games were not martial arts, and
therefore they were the people's pleasures, jealously protected by
the commoners against the authorities who considered them a
waste of time that ought to be spent in the constructive service
of the people's feudal lords.

If the grand chivalrous tournaments were often an excuse
for a holiday, the few holidays allowed to the masses were often
an excuse for a grand community game. The Shrove Tuesday
football game which is still played at Ashbourne in Derbyshire,
reputedly began in AD 217 and swiftly degenerated into a mere
excuse for a free-for-all. This was the fate of all games
descended from the original one played by Princess Nausicaa's
handmaidens twelve centuries before Christ. In 1314, the Lord
Mayor of London issued a proclamation condemning the "great
uproar in the city through certain tumults arising from great
footballs in the public fields", and forbidding "on the King's
behalf, on pain of imprisonment, that such game shall be practised within the City".

Foolish games which are no use

The shape, size and consistency of footballs around the world seem to have been remarkably similar. All footballs seem to have been bigger than balls used in racket or bat games, probably to allow more than one person to get to the ball at a time. If hundreds of people are thronging around a ball that is there to be kicked rather than thrown or hit, it soon becomes obvious that the ball should be big enough to be noticed among the throng of feet, and soft enough not to cause toes to be broken every time it is kicked. Footballs were made of bundles of rags, or odd cuts of leather, while balls for throwing, catching and hitting were made of harder materials.

By the 1360s, King Edward III banned under pain of imprisonment, "skittles, quoits, fives, football and other foolish games which are no use". Archery was not one of those "foolish games which are no use", but it was because people were spending much too much time in idle leisure and too little time practising the arts of the British longbowman that the ban took effect. Clearly the king was in no better position than his predecessor Canute in attempting to stop the incoming tide. His edict was an "order to cause proclamation to be made that every able-bodied man...on feast-days when he has leisure, shall in his sports use bows and arrows". The order explained why ball players would go to prison: archery "is almost wholly disused, and the people indulge in the games aforesaid and in other dishonest or unthrifty or idle games whereby the realm is like to be without archers".

Of course it did no good. Richard II had a try at banning football again in 1388, and there were certainly further edicts in 1414 (the year before English and Welsh longbowmen won the Battle of Agincourt) and 1477, and probably many more. After the Battle of Bosworth in 1485, even the notoriously sporting

Henry VII and Henry VIII carried on the royal tradition of banning ball games. Henry VIII went further than that, reintroducing tournaments and jousting during his reign. In 1520, Henry had attended a tournament held by the French king Francis I at the Field of the Cloth of Gold, during which at least one French knight was killed, and he obviously enjoyed the experience. It was at one of his tournaments, in 1536, that his second queen, Anne Boleyn, was arrested and in 1540 he gave another to celebrate his marriage to his fourth queen, Anne of Cleves.

The more the edicts against ball games, the less successful the authorities seemed to be. An act introduced by Henry VIII in 1541 caused landowners to be punished if they allowed football to be played on their land, and further fined if they did not train their servants in the use of a bow and arrow. Archery as a decisive weapon of war was almost a thing of the past, but the act itself remained on the statute book for three hundred and four years, until it was repealed when Sir Robert Peel was prime minister. This was, incidentally, one year after *The Boy's Treasury of Sports and Pastimes* had dismissed football in just twelve lines, describing it as "once a popular old English game". But, of course, if football was officially an illegal pastime when those words were written, it was hardly likely that an author would encourage the youth of the day to break the law. Within thirty years, for twenty-nine of which it was a legal way to spend one's leisure hours, it was to become popular again.

The beginning of official approval for ball games in Britain began in Scotland, with the game of golf. The first reference to golf in Britain is not one of approval, however. It is in a proclamation of James II of Scotland in 1457, who like his neighbour and kinsman Henry VI of England, ruled that "fute-bal and golf be utterly cryed downe and not to be used" because it was interfering with archery practice. The same edict ordered that archery practice should take place in each parish, with each man "schutte sex schottes at the least", under pain of a fine of two pennies for those who did not comply. The money thus raised was to be given "to them that cummis to the bowe-markes, to drinke". It was not really explained how the people who did not turn up would be made to part with their money in favour of those who did. It is often difficult enough to persuade people who have turned up to buy their round of drinks, but trying to get money for drinks out of people who are not there would appear to be a policy doomed to failure. That must have been the case, because the edict had to be repeated in 1471 and again in 1491, when football and golf were described as "unprofittable sports", for the umpteenth time. They may have been proving to be unprofitable as regards the defence of the realm, but they were remarkably profitable for the lawyers. All in all, it seems rather surprising that any battles were ever fought between the English and the Scots after about 1300, as both sides would obviously rather have played their own particular ball games.

By the beginning of the 16th century, the Scottish attempts to ban golf were abandoned, because King James IV took up the game. His first hooks and slices came coincidentally at a time when peace was made with England, with the signing of the Treaty of Glasgow in 1502, so anyway the need for archers to defend the realm became less urgent. He had married the daughter of Henry VII of England, so no doubt felt that family ties would overcome tribal rivalries. The ban on golf was never officially lifted by James IV, but he flouted his own law constantly. The royal records first show a purchase of golf clubs for the king in that same year, 1502, and by 1503, the whole court began to revolve around where and when a golfing party was to be arranged for the king.

The only mistake that King James IV made in his policy of switching from archery to golf was his decision to invade England in 1513. The memory of his frequent visits to England to see his wife's family, visits on which he regularly took his golf clubs, must have clouded his judgement. Henry VIII's first wife Catherine of Aragon certainly took to the game under the influence of her Scottish brother-in-law, as a letter she wrote to Cardinal Wolsey a few days before the battle of Flodden confirms, but she seems to have been the exception rather than the rule. Perhaps King James thought that the swords-into-ploughshares, or rather bows-into-golf-clubs, policy was further advanced in England than in Scotland, and that therefore he could hope to catch a weakened English army unprepared for the Scottish onslaught, but it turned out to be a mistake. Marching south at the head of his army, he swept into England on 22 August, quickly took Norham and several other castles, but came to a halt at Flodden, a ridge on the Cheviot Hills just south of the River Tweed. On 9 September 1513, just at the turn of the cricket and football seasons in years to come, the Scots king, followed fairly closely by his army, swept down the hill and took on the might of his brother-in-law's army, led by the Earl of Surrey. But at the end of the day, it was the Earl of Surrey who was over the moon and James IV who was as sick as Monty Python's Norwegian Blue parrot. The English archers had once again won the day. It proved to be a transient victory for the English army. The first royal golfer had been killed along with perhaps ten thousand of his countrymen, but within a hundred years, both his family and his game would have taken over the rest of Britain.

FOOLISH GAMES WHICH ARE NO USE

The spread of golf from Scotland into England was not just a simple geographical advance; it was also a social phenomenon, and for this the Battle of Flodden must take some responsibility. As all Scottish schoolchildren know, the flower of Scotland's nobility were killed at Flodden, a class slaughter that has no real parallel in British history. But golf was already the people's game in Scotland, so the loss of so many great warrior lords had little effect on the further growth of the game there. In England, however, golf had been introduced as a court pastime, and it retained its image as a game for the upper classes for years to come.

Throughout the 16th century, there are frequent references to the growth of the game of golf in Scotland, generally with the approval of the authorities of both church and state. James IV's son was barely one year old when his father died and he became James V, but legend has it that he was taught golf at the insistence of his father. His main contribution to the game was the establishment of a royal links at Gosford, east of Edinburgh on the Firth of Forth, and the issuance of an edict that only wooden-headed clubs were to be used on the royal course, as iron heads cut too many divots and destroyed too many golf balls. This shows, if nothing else, that club-making was already becoming a specialist and sophisticated art four and half centuries ago. When James V died aged only thirty in 1542, his six-day-old daughter Mary became queen. By then, the tradition of royal golf was firmly established. Even when Mary went to school in France, she took her golf clubs with her, and it is quite possible that the word "caddie" comes from the French *cadet*, after the young students in Paris who were obliged to carry her clubs for her.

Golf played an indirect part in Mary's death, as it had with her grandfather. When her cousin, the consistently unsporting

Queen Elizabeth of England, eventually found an excuse to bring Mary to trial, one of the most damning pieces of evidence against her was that in 1567, after the death of her second husband the Earl of Darnley, she "played golf and pall mall in the fields beside Seton", and then afterwards, instead of standing at the bar embellishing the details of her thirty-foot putt for a half on the sixteenth as any self-respecting golfer should have done, she "did abuse her body with Bothwell". Guilty as charged, m'lud; on with the black cap and off with her head.

While Mary was abusing her body with Bothwell in Scotland, in England a young schoolmaster was reaching the revolutionary and subversive conclusion that public sports and boisterous exercise were not such a bad thing after all. Richard Mulcaster, the schoolmaster in question, was born in 1530 or 1531 (or maybe even 1532), making him ten years or so older than the doomed Mary, and was educated at Eton. He was thus very much aware of Juvenal's view that "*orandum est ut sit mens sana in corpore sano*", but as another of his major themes in life was that English should be the language of learning rather than Latin, he was much more likely to express the sentiment in English: "Your prayer should be for a healthy mind in a healthy body." Mulcaster became the first headmaster of the Merchant Taylors' School in London, which was founded in 1561. He wrote two books, in 1581 and 1582, the first of which rejoiced in the snappy title of *The Positions wherein those Primitive Circumstances be examined, which are Necessary for the Training Up of Children, either for Skill in their Booke, or Health in their Bodie*, usually shortened these days to *Positions*. By the time he wrote his second book, one of the first school textbooks, he had learnt the art of the shorter title and called it *The First Part of the Elementarie*. He never wrote the second part.

Sporting brutality deplored by John Bull, a cartoon from *Punch* in 1888. Football has always walked a thin line between the civilising impulses of muscular Christianity and the more ancient traditions of all-out war with a ball

The most remarkable feature of *Positions*, however, was not in that it was written in English but the message that physical exercise is of educational value, and his proposal for organised games at school. Mulcaster was writing at the same time as the puritanical and prudish Philip Stubbes, who in his *Anatomy of Abuses in the Realm of England* put forward the view that "any exercise which withdraweth us from godliness, either upon the

Sabbath or any other day else is wicked and to be forbidden". Yet Mulcaster, far from wanting to forbid what Stubbes described as "a friendly kind of fight [rather] than a play or recreation", argued the merits of a wide range of athletic pursuits, covering in forty-five chapters such particular sports as "wrastling" (Chapter 17), "fensing" (Chapter 18) and "top and scourge" (Chapter 18). Walking, running, leaping, swimming, riding, hunting and shooting all had their own chapters, too, as did "loude and soft reading", "holding the breath" and "daunsing, why it is blamed, and how delivered from blame". But the chapter that has interested researchers most over the years has been Chapter 27, "Of The Ball".

In Chapter 27, Mulcaster states unreservedly that ball games are of great value to the whole community because they help preserve the health of the masses who take part. Yet he talks of only a limited range of ball games, and conspicuously does not make any clear reference to either golf or cricket, which at the time were certainly being played by both men and boys. "Three kindes shall content me...wherein all the properties of their balles, and all the effectes of their exercises, be most evidently seene. The hand ball, the footeball, the armeball.

"The litle hand ball whether it be of some softer stuffe, and used by the hand alone, or of some harder, and used with the rackette, whether by tennice play with an other, or against a wall alone, to exercise the bodie with both the handes, in everie kinde of motion, that concerneth any, or all the other exercises, is generally noted, to be one of the best exercises and the greatest preservations of health." So we know that real tennis, rackets and something rather like fives were all well-known and widely played games in Mulcaster's time. Fives as it is played today exists in two major variations, Eton fives and Rugby fives, although there is also Winchester fives which is barely played outside Winchester. Both Eton and Rugby fives involve a small, hard leather ball which is struck with the hand (wearing a padded glove) against a wall. The name "fives" probably comes from the five fingers on the hand, "a bunch of fives" as common slang has it, although there is an alternative theory that it gained its name when it was demonstrated to Queen Elizabeth I in 1591, with teams of five a side. On that occasion "ten of my lord of Hartford's servants, all Somersetshire men, in a square green court before Her Majesty's window, did lay up lines, squaring out the form of a tennis court, and making a crosse line in the middle." The game these ten men played was a five-a-side version of "bord and cord (as they term it) to so great liking of Her Highness". What the men were playing was not fives, though, it was more like tennis or the French *jeu de paume*. Dr Samuel Johnson described fives in his *Dictionary* of 1755 as "a kind of play with a bowl", a "bowl" being by his definition "a round mass which may be rolled along the ground". But Dr Johnson was no sportsman.

As for "armeball", it seems that Mulcaster was thinking of a game not unlike pelota, which we know was being played in contemporary Spain, because Cervantes (1547–1616) mentions it in his writings. (As an aside, Charles Jarvis's English translation of *Don Quixote* caused a brief flurry of consternation among sports historians. The sentence describing Basilius as a "*gran jugador de pelota*" was translated as a "great cricket player" leading some readers to conclude that cricket was played in 16th-century Spain). However, Mulcaster's armeball was, he claims, invented in Naples "not many yeares ago".

"The arme in this is fensed with a wodden brace, as the shin in the other with some other thing for meeting with a shrew." Clearly, the invention of protective sportswear dates back at least four hundred years, with arm pads in a wooden brace, shin pads and "some other thing for meeting with a shrew". Is this the first recorded mention of the abdominal protector?

Mulcaster obviously approves of handball and armball, but seems most in favour of football. "Footeball strengtheneth and brawneth the whole body," he writes. Mulcaster, like Stubbes and all other commentators of the time, agreed that uncontrolled street football was not a good thing, so he came up with the remarkable suggestion that "if one stand by, which can judge of the play and is judge of the parties and hath authority to commande in the place, all those inconveniences…will never entermedle in the matter, neither shall there be complaint where there is no cause. Some smaller number…sorted into sides and standings, not meeting with their bodies so boisterously to trie their strength: not shouldring or shuffing one another so barbarously…may use football for as much good to the body."

In those few sentences, Mulcaster invented the referee and the concept of equal numbers on each side, although hindsight would prove he was wearing rose-tinted spectacles if he thought that the presence of the referee would eliminate "complaint where there is no cause". Still, the concept of a game regulated by an impartial judge, and with far fewer participants than in the street games, was way ahead of its time. It would be three hundred years before anybody took him seriously, and probably three hundred years before anybody realised the ideas were not original to Mulcaster. He had read *De Arte Gymnastica* by the Italian Girolamo Mercuriali, which had been published in Venice in 1569.

As Mercuriali writes, "the most of these notes, which I have alleaged, were given in Italie, Greece and Spaine". The main difference between the ball games that were played in Italy, Greece and Spain and those played in Mulcaster's London was that in Europe, the games were played by the nobility, but Mulcaster was writing about games for the people, "the common weale". Pelota was not at this time a game for the masses, while the contemporary Italian version of football, calcio, was certainly a game for gentlemen. The game was centred in Florence, but was not for the masses: "no artisans or servants, but honoured soldiers, gentlemen, lords and princes. Those chosen to play calcio will be gentlemen from eighteen to forty-five years, or more or less according to temperament, of good repute, well regarded and agreeable."[3] The game was an obsession with 16th-century Florentines. It was even played in 1530 by two teams of twenty-five men, one team wearing white and one team wearing green (taking up the tradition of sporting colours from the battlefield and the tournaments) when the city of Florence was under siege from forty thousand soldiers of the army of the Emperor Charles V.

Whatever the health-giving aspects of football may have been, as argued by Mulcaster and others, they did not work for the defending army of the besieged city. The siege was successful, the Florentine republic was overthrown and the dukedom of Florence was established by the Medici family. The first duke celebrated his betrothal to the Austrian princess Margherita two years after the siege with what else but a game of calcio. The word calcio is still in use today to describe what we now know as association football, but the two games are not all that similar. Cynical non-Italians might suspect the word is used simply to claim the Italians invented the game first.

Richard Mulcaster was a lone voice crying in the wilderness, even though he himself went on from Merchant Taylors' to become headmaster of St Paul's, and presumably he put his theories of organised sports into practice at both schools. The prevailing mood was still that ball games were a lawless disruption of the peace of the commonwealth. There were many other schools founded in the latter years of Queen Elizabeth's reign and in the first years of the Stuart dynasty, but Mulcaster's ideas did not take root. Harrow school was founded in 1571, and the statutes (drawn up in 1590, after Mulcaster had published his ideas) did indeed prescribe physical exercise for the pupils. However, they were specifically limited to running, archery, driving a top and tossing a hand ball, with no mention of organised team games. The same was true of Charterhouse (founded in 1611) and Dulwich College (founded 1619). So if the school governors and head teachers of the day knew of Mulcaster's ideas, they chose deliberately to ignore them.

The 17th and early 18th centuries were not times when people paid much attention to the virtues of ball games. Although there is plenty of evidence of the masses and the nobility diverting themselves throughout the land and across all of Europe chasing balls or causing them to be chased, there is little sign at this stage of the virtues of ball games as events to enjoy watching. With the exception of the ancient Olympic Games and to a lesser extent the games of calcio in Florence, sports were participatory events, a means of enjoying oneself in an unruly throng (if you sided with Philip Stubbes and the moralists of the age) or a means of keeping fit and healthy (if Richard Mulcaster was to be believed). Nobody seemed to consider ball games as a spectator event. This was surprising in view of the success of the tournaments of earlier centuries, and of archery contests and the like which continued even though the heyday of the longbowman was passing. Of course, the big games of football in the streets of the towns and the villages were spectator events to the extent that people in the way could hardly avoid witnessing the hurly-burly, but there were no admission charges, no promoters looking for a quick profit, and no professional players – yet.

When people played golf or cricket or football or tennis in those days, it was for their own pleasure. What is more, the roads and transport systems were so rudimentary that any game regularly played in one area was not likely to spread very far beyond its natural boundaries. So there was no need at first to make general country- or county-wide rules of how any game should be played, and there was certainly no concept of national sport or enough public interest in any of the various ball games to create national sporting heroes.

The first athletic activities to create a nation-wide spectator interest were not ball games. They were horse-racing and boxing, both of which are of limited interest as participant sports, the one because it has always required wealth to own and train a good racehorse, and the other because not many people enjoy having their faces and ribs broken in single combat, especially in the days before the eighth Marquess of Queensberry (1844–1900). Both horse-racing and boxing, however, are very exciting to watch. They are very simple to understand and appeal to basic instincts. They also, usually, provide a clear-cut winner to each contest.

After the Civil War and the eventual restoration of the monarchy in 1660, once peace had been established long enough for the great lords to have leisure time on their hands, these simple ingredients of both racing and boxing led inevitably to the beginnings of a national industry. The national industry in question was gambling. The noble lords were not sufficiently noble to enjoy the race for its own sake, nor the noble art of watching two people thump the daylights out of each other with their bare fists just for the aesthetic pleasure it brings. They wanted to continue the habits of many generations by wagering that their horse or their man would outrun or outfight their rival's. The contest was always worth watching, but it was even more worth betting on.

The joining of the ancient habit of betting with the more modern habit of organised sports events created two new professions. It gave us the professional spectator, who by placing a bet on the outcome could feel involved. More than just a mere onlooker, he would learn to rejoice in the name of "sportsman" even if he had never actually done anything more strenuous than raising a tankard to his lips, or telling the world exactly how fast his horse could run or how hard his man could punch. But Richard Mulcaster had noted the virtues of "lowd speaking, how necessarie, and how proper an exercise it is for a scholler", so our gamblers could be known as scholars as well as sportsmen.

Gambling also gave us the professional sportsman. In the days of the ancient Greeks and Romans, the point of sport was, in Mulcaster's words, "to winne some wager, to beare awaie the prise, to be wondered at of the world, or to set foorth the solemnities of their festivall service, and ceremonies in the honour of their idoles." Gambling was a part of the equation, but so were "their idoles", who could live entirely on the glory and the financial rewards that came with their public success. By the early 18th century in Britain, because gamblers needed sure things to bet on, there were professional jockeys and professional prize fighters, too.

Throughout sporting history, professionalism and betting have grown together. Where there is no betting, there is no professionalism, and it does not take a particularly observant sports follower to notice that as we reach the third millennium, there are no amateur sports left. In the final thirty years or so of this century, we have seen the last great international sports surrender to the onslaught of the professional: tennis, rugby union, cricket and even the Olympic Games have abandoned their links with the amateur ideal. The only difference today is that the professional sportsman is now a social lion, much higher up the pecking order than he ever was in the early days of professional sport. This is a very new development, though, which in Britain can be traced to just a few decades ago when professional sportsmen like Len Hutton, Jack Hobbs, Gordon Richards and Stanley Matthews received knighthoods. At the same time, the money paid to professional sportsmen underwent several massive increases.

The first recorded boxing match in Britain was a fight in January 1681 between the Duke of Albemarle's butcher and his butler, probably at the Albemarle family seat in Essex. The result of this fight between two of his Lordship's servants is not known, but we can be sure that the Duke and his cronies had some money on one fighter or the other. This fight took place fourteen years before the birth of James Figg, who was to create the public sport of boxing almost on his own.

Figg, a native of Thame in Oxfordshire, was a champion swordsman and cudgel fighter as well as a bare-knuckle boxer, and in 1719 he set up his own school of arms in what is now Tottenham Court Road, London. It was in 1727 that he was able to declare himself champion, after beating a pipemaker from Gravesend called Ned Sutton. Although he has been described as "boxing's first champion", he actually won the fight with a combination of fists, sword and cudgel, and a lack of rules which made the sport extremely dangerous and rather more popular with the gamblers than the participants. Nevertheless, James Figg's school grew, and among his pupils was the Bristol-born John Broughton (1704–1789), now known as the "father of boxing".

Figg ran a boxing booth at Southwark Fair – Figg's Great Tiled Booth on the Bowling Green, Southwark – where he staged most of his fights. Pierce Egan, the 19th century sporting journalist, described Southwark Fair as "an uncommon scene of attraction to the inhabitants in, and contiguous to, London, from the various sports and pastimes which were exhibited by its versatility of performers. Boxing and cudgelling were strong features among the other amusements: refinement was not so well understood then as at the present period."[4] Despite the regular attendance of many of the great and aristocratic names of the day, from the king to Dr Samuel Johnson, Jonathan Swift and William Hogarth, the lack of any order eventually led to the demise of both the Fair and Figg's version of prizefighting. "Boxing and cudgelling," reported Egan, "degenerated into down-right ferocity and barbarity at this fair, from the drunkenness and inequality of the combatants, and the various artifices adopted to get money, which at last became so disgusting, that it was declared a public nuisance." In 1743, three years after the death of James Figg and the same year in which James Broughton drew up the first set of rules for boxing, Southwark Fair was closed.

Figg and Broughton reputedly first met in the ring in 1733, at the end of a programme at Southwark Fair, promoted by Figg, which included the first international fight, between another Figg pupil, Bob Whittaker, and the Italian Tito Alberto di Carini. Carini, who rejoiced in the professional nickname of "The Venetian Gondolier", had been brought to London by the

Earl of Bath, and among the other spectators at this fight were King George II and Frederick, Prince of Wales, both of whom were likely to have made a large wager on the outcome. Seventeen years later, when John Broughton lost his ten-year hold on the championship title to Jack Slack, his loss was reported to have cost the Duke of Cumberland, son of King George II and victor over the Scots at Culloden in 1746, a massive ten thousand pounds in bets. Despite earning the enmity of His Royal Highness the Butcher of Culloden, who thought that Broughton had thrown the fight, Broughton lived on until the year of the French Revolution, 1789, and was finally buried in Westminster Abbey. Egan described Broughton as "athletic and commanding ...Six feet, wanting an inch, in height; and fourteen stone, or thereabouts, in weight." His superiority as a boxer at his peak was never in doubt: "most of his competitors, who were compelled to give in from their exhausted and beaten state, had the mortification to behold Broughton scarcely touched, and to appear with as much cheerfulness and indifference as if he had never been engaged in a set-to."

By the time that Figg and Broughton were bringing a tinge of organisation and order to bare-knuckle fighting, and dancing to the tune of their rich and reckless sponsors, horse-racing was also becoming a more regular public spectacle. There had been a racecourse at Chester since King Henry VIII's day, and the Newmarket Gold Cup was first competed for a century later in 1634, by which time Robert Burton (1577–1640) had noted that so much money was being wagered on horse races that "many gentlemen by such means gallop themselves out of their fortunes".[5] It was King Charles II who established Newmarket as the headquarters of racing and who began a tradition of royal involvement in horse-racing which continues to this day.

Charles II's horse won the Gold Cup in 1671, and the gambling fever which accompanied the first glimmerings of organised racing grew so rapidly and so chaotically that the nation's economy (and more pertinently, its social hierarchy) was seen to be threatened. Parliament therefore passed a law to prevent creditors from collecting on horse-racing wagers in excess of ten pounds, which leads us to the inevitable conclusion that most of the members of Parliament at that time must have had outstanding gambling debts well above the ten-pound limit.

The royal family were not only supporters of racing and boxing. Frederick, Prince of Wales, who had attended the boxing match between Bob Whittaker and the Venetian Gondolier in 1733, was the eldest son of King George II. He had been born in Hanover in 1707, before his grandfather succeeded to the British throne. He arrived in England in December 1728, and was created Prince of Wales on his twenty-second birthday, 6 January 1729. He was by all accounts a deeply unpleasant man. His main interests were women and gambling. At first he limited his gambling to the sports that he could readily understand, horse-racing and boxing, but he soon discovered the gambling possibilities of cricket, a sport he had apparently been introduced to as a boy in Germany. For many of his contemporaries, Frederick's only redeeming feature was that he wanted to be English, even if he wasn't.

From the early 1730s, he attended many great matches, especially those involving the Surrey XI whose patron he became. Surrey County Cricket Club still wear the Prince of Wales's feathers on their caps and their ground in Kennington is owned by the Prince of Wales (in his capacity as the Duke of Cornwall), a link with the sons of monarchs that continues two hundred and fifty years on. Prince Frederick almost always had a large fortune riding on the result of any cricket match he watched. His influence in the short term may not have been very good for the growth of the game, but in the longer term, it could be argued that his interest in the game, whatever his ulterior motives might have been, created a climate of national awareness of cricket, which could only help the game to grow. Unfortunately, where Frederick led, the country did not necessarily follow. Frederick and his father King George II "were constantly at variance on financial and other matters",[6] which was not surprising given the sums he was wagering on the results of cricket matches, and in 1737 he was banished from the court.

The famous poem 'Cricket' by James Love (the pseudonym of James Dance 1722–1774) about the cricket match between Kent and All England played at the Honourable Artillery Company's Ground in London on 18 June 1744, includes the lines:

> While the drooping player invok'd the Gods,
> The busy better calculates his Odds.
> Swift round the plain, in buzzing murmurs run.
> I'll hold you ten to four, Kent – Done, Sir – Done.

This sport, which Love invokes as:

> Hail, cricket! Glorious, manly, British Game!
> First of all Sports! Be first alike in Fame!

was in reality not much more than another excuse for gambling. It is interesting to note, though, that the earliest set of rules for the game which survives today is dated 1744. The match at the HAC ground was so important that there had to be not only a heroic ode to celebrate it, but also an agreed set of rules.

Cricket under the Prince of Wales's baleful influence attracted not only aristocratic benefactors but also the dregs of the underworld. In 1731, there were reports of fights among spectators at cricket matches, in one of which the Duke of Richmond was attacked by a mob. At least that proved there were enough spectators at these games to start a fight serious enough to attract the attention of the writers of the time. When Frederick Prince of Wales died in 1751, probably as a result of being hit by a cricket ball, few people mourned him, although the Surrey XI were now short of a patron.

His epitaph was poetic, too, although the author wisely remained anonymous.

Here lies Fred, who was alive and is dead.
Had it been his father, I had much rather.
Had it been his brother, still better than another.
Had it been his sister, no one would have missed her.
Had it been the whole generation, still better for the nation:
But since 'tis only Fred, who was alive and is dead
There's no more to be said.

Neither sport nor the Royal House of Hanover was much affected by his untimely death. But Fred was in his way a revolutionary in sporting history. Ball games had, as we have seen, been regarded largely as anti-establishment events, pastimes which lured the common people away from practising the martial arts so necessary to the defence of the realm. They were also seen as opportunities for disorganised – and therefore subversive – gatherings of too many people in one place at one time to be for the good of the community, or at least for the good of the feudal lord of the community. Crowds, even when asked to sing "Abide With Me" on the terraces at Wembley Stadium, do not always do what is asked of them. But "poor Fred", so unaware of the truly English way of doing things however hard he tried, was the aristocrat with common tastes, and therefore a misfit at both social levels. He united the masters and the servants in one thing: their contempt for him. But he did bring the games he loved to the centre of society, and that had a huge bearing on their future development. He was a forerunner of the sporting parsons of the next century in the way he espoused the common sports of the proletariat (who as a class did not really exist until Marx told us they did a century after Prince Fred died). His motives were ignoble where the muscular Christians were noble, but the effect was the same: before too long all sports would be open to all people.

"MORAL AND INTELLECTUAL
EXCELLENCE"

By 1750, ball games were alive rather than dead, but only just. There was real tennis and other indoor ball games similar to fives, there were outdoor sports like cricket and golf which had a modicum of organisation and the beginnings of a nation-wide popularity, and there were the people's ball games, like football, which existed in a hundred varieties, none of which were properly codified and all of which invoked official displeasure. Sport was still a tiny part of the average Briton's life, and ball games just a fraction of that tiny part.

Ball games are, of course, a pursuit mainly for young people and in the 18th and early 19th century, this meant young men. Young women were not supposed to take exercise, except in dancing. Very few women in this era hunted; they were expected to be docile and remain indoors. In 1801 Wordsworth dedicated a poem to "A Young Lady, who had been Reproached for Taking Long Walks in the Country", a fate that also befell Elizabeth Bennett in *Pride and Prejudice* when she walked three miles to Netherfield, where she arrived "with weary ankles, dirty stockings and a face glowing with warmth and exercise". Miss Bingley, needless to say, "held her in contempt for it". In this, the fictional Miss Bingley was directly at odds with her name-

Suitable sporting dress in an age when it was not proper for a lady to perspire in public – from the *Girl's Own* paper, 1906

sake of seventy years later, Blanche Bingley, ladies' singles champion at Wimbledon six times from 1886, whose face was often glowing with warmth and exercise. Even in the 1880s while Blanche Bingley was perspiring so freely on the centre court at Wimbledon, the amateur champion golfer Horace Hutchinson was proclaiming that women would never be able to play golf properly, and in 1902 Baron Pierre de Coubertin outlined the role of women at his Olympic Games in one short sentence: "Women have but one task, that of crowning the winner with garlands." Young men play sports, women just admire them from a respectful distance.

The link between sport and education, made by Richard Mulcaster two hundred years earlier, was still tenuous in the reign of the mad King George III, son of the unlamented Frederick, Prince of Wales. At the turn of the century, secondary education was divided, according to the historian G.M. Trevelyan, into three kinds of institution. Firstly there were the "public" schools, which numbered only about ten at the time (Eton, Winchester, Westminster, Christ's Hospital, Charterhouse, St Paul's, Merchant Taylors', Harrow, Rugby and Shrewsbury) and which were confined to the home counties with the exceptions of Rugby and Shrewsbury which were in the Midlands. Then there were private academies "where the unfashionable Dissenting middle class received a more scientific and modern education under better discipline".[1] These schools had been made possible by a 1779 Act of Parliament which had for the first time made it lawful for Protestant Nonconformists to become teachers. Finally, there were the endowed grammar schools, which were in a poor state at the end of the 18th century, in common with most public institutions of the time. However, sports were played at many of these schools, even though there was almost no official approval for them.

Students at the major public schools, as we learn from a document that describes the games played at Eton in 1766, enjoyed many different sports and pastimes in their free time, with or without official approval. The Eton list is a very long one, including cricket (at the time unquestionably the most fashionable of the ball games), fives, hopscotch, marbles, kites, battledores and hoops. There were also references to more obscure games (to our eyes) such as "shirking walls", "scrambling walls", "bally cally", "conquering lobs", "puss in the corner", "cloyster and glyer gigs", "starecap" and "hurtlecap". The rules, if any, of these games do not survive. The Eton scholars also played "goals" and "headers", which may well indicate some early form of football, although goals could equally well describe a form of hockey and headers may well be a reference to diving head first into a swimming hole.

The list is most remarkable for what it did not include: hunting, boating, racing, fishing, tennis and billiards for a start. These were all sports which were available to the young men when they ventured into Eton or Windsor. Boats were available on the Thames and the college had its own rod-maker. Boys could hire horses, and they could visit the races at Datchet or Ascot. At the public houses in the town, most notably The Christopher, they could play billiards and they could drink. There were also the added amusements of cock-fighting, bull- and bear-baiting and even a public hanging now and again to keep the pupils happy.

At Charterhouse, originally founded as a charitable institution in 1611, they had a song which was first sung in 1794, showing that sport was a central part of the students' lives:

> I challenge all the men alive
> To say they e'er were gladder
> Than boys all striving who should kick
> Most wind out of the bladder.

At Rugby School at that time, we know that exercise was part of the curriculum. They played cricket, some kind of football and they went swimming. They also spent much of their time fishing and shooting, much to the displeasure of the local landowners and farmers. Rugby School was not unusual in inciting some section of the local populace to complain. Sports were part of the students' lives; they did not care if they were not approved or even tolerated, because they paid scant attention to what they were told to do. Overall, discipline in the public schools was virtually non-existent. Riots were commonplace throughout the latter part of the eighteenth century, so much so that King George III's standard question whenever he met any Eton boys was, "Have you had a good rebellion lately?"

The schools of this time had a teaching staff of perhaps only one teacher to every thirty boys, and even then the teaching staff had little responsibility for, or eagerness to impose, discipline. Thus they were organisations run by young men on the principle of brute force, who practised extraordinarily cruel forms of bullying, inflicting tortures on the smaller boys as though it was a natural part of growing up. It was not only within the school bounds that the boys were liable to face physical danger. A Westminster schoolboy on a half holiday in the 1770s was considered to be at as much risk as a midshipman on shore leave of "being married to some slut in the back parlour of a public house"[2] but any attempt to prevent Westminster

A cricket match between Eton and Winchester Colleges, 1864. Organised sport brought discipline and a concept of fair play to the often brutal and riotous English public school

schoolboys from running that particular risk would have been met with ferocity by the boys themselves. Many of the school rebellions came about because some such small limit was imposed on the freedom of the pupils to do exactly as they chose with impunity, or maybe because the governors or the headmaster chose to act without first consulting the boys. In case it should be imagined that these riots were exaggerated or were few and far between, an authoritative list shows four riots at Winchester between 1770 and 1793 (one because the headmaster decided, without consulting his prefects, that a saint's day should be a school day rather than a holiday), three at Eton and three at Rugby in the same period. In 1818, a rebellion at Winchester grew so serious that the headmaster had to call in the local militia, who arrived with fixed bayonets to put down the insurrection. A schoolmaster wrote in 1806 that "the youth at Eton are dissipated gentlemen; those at Winchester dissipated with a little of the blackguard; and those at St Paul's the most depraved of all." Sydney Smith, the author, priest and founder of *The Edinburgh Review* who was also an alumnus of Winchester, wrote at the time that public schools "only prevent men from being corrupted by the world by corrupting them before their entry into the world". They were not the most obvious breeding grounds for the concept of "fair play" that would be the ideal for Victorian gentlemen by the end of the century.

Dr John Keate (1773–1852) was a clergyman and headmaster of Eton from 1809 until 1834. While one authority states that "under him the tone and character of the school were greatly improved",[3] he is best remembered for the quantity and the savagery of his floggings. Though he was barely five feet tall, he thought nothing of flogging tens of pupils at a time. On one celebrated occasion he flogged all seventy-two pupils in the sixth and upper fifth forms for cheating in Latin composition. These were public executions. "It was a grand scene in the library. The floor was covered with victims...The lower boys were delighted to see their masters whipped."[4] In 1832 he flogged eighty boys, beating them in relays through the night, after a disagreement arising from the expulsion of a boy who had refused to be flogged. The last serious rebellion, which resulted in five expulsions and the usual round of mass floggings, was at Marlborough in 1851. Obviously, for the schoolmasters and pupils of the early 19th century, there were far more important things to do than organise games of football or cricket.

Yet it was from this highly unsatisfactory breeding ground that much of the impetus for the organisation of our ball games came. Within thirty years of the riots, William Webb Ellis had famously (although almost certainly apocryphally) picked up the ball and run with it, and sport as a manly and virtuous pastime was becoming the mainstay of the English education system. How come?

The most important element in this transformation was one man – Dr Thomas Arnold, appointed headmaster of Rugby School in 1828. Dr Arnold was not in any particular way interested in sports, but he transformed the way the public schools worked, and this in turn created the right conditions for sport to flourish. He was also well aware of the social changes going on around him beyond the boundaries of Rugby School; when he saw the first London to Birmingham train pass beneath him as he stood on the bridge above, he said that he rejoiced to see it, "and to think that feudality is gone forever". The coming of the railways was not just a death blow to feudalism, however. It was also one of the fairy godmothers to the birth of national sports. Now that people would be able to travel more easily, more quickly and more widely than ever before, the opportunities to organise national sporting events grew much better.

Dr Arnold's reforms were mainly in the discipline of his school. He was of the opinion that "it is not necessary that this should be a school of three hundred or one hundred and fifty boys, but it is necessary that it should be a school of Christian gentlemen". He defined the purpose of education to be "a union of moral and intellectual excellence", but made no mention of physical excellence. He was not a sports enthusiast; in fact one of his first actions on being appointed headmaster was to get rid of the school's pack of hounds (some reports suggest that he had them put down, which seems an unnecessary cruelty for such a moral Christian gentleman), and to make it clear that hunting, shooting and fishing would not be tolerated at Rugby.

But he tolerated ball games, which is more than can be said for other headmasters of the time. A cricket match between Charterhouse and Westminster in 1794 was reported in a newspaper as being "City Of London against City of Westminster", almost certainly because the boys taking part would have been flogged if it had been discovered what they were intending to do, or had done.[5] Dr Keate's predecessor at Eton, Dr Heath, flogged boys who played against Westminster in 1796. Forty years later, Dr Arnold stood on the touchline and cheered his boys on when they played sports, but he never allowed their games an official place in the curriculum.

However, the academic and disciplinary reforms he put in place at Rugby very quickly enhanced the reputation of the school, with the result that in the first half of the century only Rugby and Eton among the public schools retained anything like the numbers of pupils they had attracted at the turn of the century. Even Eton suffered, with pupil numbers slipping from 627 in the 1820s to 486 in 1834. Charterhouse, which had been teaching over 400 students, was down to 99 in 1835, while Harrow could boast only 69 pupils in 1844. Westminster's numbers fell from 324 in 1818, the year they refused to play Charterhouse at cricket because they considered that Charterhouse was not truly a public school, to 100 in 1835, but Rugby, which had been a prosperous foundation before Arnold arrived, flourished. The result was that Arnold needed to recruit new teaching staff, and it was these teachers who more enthusiastically espoused the ideas of Richard Mulcaster, partly perhaps because Dr Arnold himself did not, and this was the one area where his staff could establish their own authority and impose their own personalities on the boys. Many of these teachers went on to found schools of their own, as did some of Dr Arnold's pupils who were inspired by his example to become schoolmasters themselves. For example, it was Dr C.J. Vaughan, a pupil of Dr Arnold's, who took over as headmaster at Harrow in 1845, when numbers were at their lowest, and added 400 pupils to the roll over the next fourteen years. Although he was reputed to have hated games during his days at Rugby, by the time he was running Harrow, he wrote that "it is thought almost discreditable not to play, and play well, at some game".

In the latter part of the 19th century, there was a huge explosion in the number of "public" schools, many of which had headmasters who had taught or been taught at Rugby. Such men as George Cotton, who came to Marlborough from teaching at Rugby in 1851, introduced organised games as part of the official curriculum. Edward White Benson was assistant master at Rugby before becoming the first headmaster of Wellington College in 1859, and eventually going on to become Archbishop of Canterbury. John Percival became the first headmaster of Clifton in 1862, after many years teaching at Rugby. John Collis, a Rugby teacher who went on to become headmaster at Bromsgrove in 1843 is generally reckoned to have been the first headmaster to play football at school. He played the Rugby version, of course. As the official history of the school records: "he was a plump man and was fond of catching the ball on the bounce. But he never ran. He stood stock still with the ball in his arms, and the players swarmed round him like bees."[6]

Philpotts at Bedford, Lee at King Edward's Birmingham and other Rugby men at Sedburgh, Fettes and Haileybury, among others, also spread the word of "a union of moral and intellectual excellence", but added the physical element to it. Sport was beginning to be accepted as a positive influence on the education of Christian gentlemen. The first school gymnasium was built at Uppingham in 1859, followed by Radley (founded in 1847) in 1860. Even the architecture of schools was changing as muscular Christianity was born.

The origin of the term "muscular Christianity" is hard to pin down, but its meaning is clear: it is what the Reverend James Pycroft was describing when he wrote in his epic *The Cricket Field* in 1851, "gambling and cudgel-playing insensibly disappear before a manly recreation which draws the labourer from the dark haunts of vice and misery to the open common". It is the philosophy of *mens sana in corpore sano* – a healthy mind in a healthy body – and it is what drove the upper-class, inner-city priests of the 1870s and 1880s to create church football teams for the moral uplift of their parishioners. In the public schools after Dr Arnold's time, the philosophy had swept all before it. Nobody argued against the idea that vigorous and often masochistic sporting efforts were good for the soul.

By 1840, Eton College had even appointed their own cricket professional, Samuel Redgate of Nottingham. Redgate was scarcely a fine example of Christianity, although he was certainly muscular. He was one of the first, and certainly the fastest, of the new "round-arm" bowlers, and in 1839 he had taken a hat-trick playing for England against Kent, then the strongest county side in the country. He clean bowled the great Fuller Pilch with the second ball of the over, he clean bowled the equally great Alfred Mynn with the third ball, and finished the over by doing the same to William Stearman, a Kent professional who had played occasionally for England select elevens. The Reverend James Pycroft, a chronicler of the early years of cricket, records that after each wicket, Redgate drank a large glass of brandy, so perhaps it was fortunate that an over consisted of only four balls in those days. The rest of Redgate's career was one of fast bowling and fast living. He drank himself to death in 1851 at the age of forty.

In that same year, Winchester appointed the great William Lillywhite as their coach. Even at the age of fifty-nine, he was able to help the boys to such an extent that their results improved immediately. It would not be long before all schools hired professional coaches for their boys, a career opportunity opening up for retired cricketers who otherwise would have had no chance to continue doing the only thing they had ever been good at. Several of them would prove, like Sam Redgate, to be as fond of the bottle as of cricket, but overall, the improvement in the standard of cricket in the public schools was in a direct relationship with the number of professional coaches employed there. Without them, the sustained rise in cricket's popularity in the latter part of the 19th century might never have happened.

However, more factors than orderly schools and better communications were required to create and encourage a national sporting culture. The voyage of the *Endeavour* and the conquests of Clive; the storming of the Bastille in 1789; the madness of King George III and the frivolity of his son the Prince Regent; and the passing of the Factory Acts of 1833 and 1847 also had important parts to play.

Captain James Cook, sometimes described with a degree of poetic licence as the first Yorkshireman to captain England in Australia, took the *Endeavour* to Australia in 1769, when he was forty-one years old, a couple of years older than two other Yorkshiremen who took teams to Australia, Len Hutton in 1954–1955 and Ray Illingworth in 1970–1971. Cook, however, did not bring back the Ashes as Hutton and Illingworth did. He did not even play cricket down under, although his men almost certainly did, and in so doing introduced sport to the Australians. Cook's tours took place scarcely a decade after Clive had claimed much of the Indian sub-continent for the British Empire, and Wolfe had won Quebec from France. Suddenly the map of the world was turning red.

The sudden expansion of the British Empire, even despite the loss of the United States in the 1770s, meant that there was a great need for administrators. Young men with imperial ideals began to travel overseas, taking with them not only their morals and their innate feelings of superiority, but also their love of games. Cricket, the game most associated with Imperial Britain, was first recorded in Canada in 1785, having been played in the United States since at least the 1740s. It was played in South Africa before the end of the 18th century, and also in India. It was only a couple of years later that we know organised cricket was being played in Australia, and in 1806, there were reports of cricket being played by British prisoners of war in the Argentine, after an unsuccessful military expedition to the River Plate. This was a few years after the first reports of cricket in Barbados. Cricket in New Zealand did not get going until a few years after that; the first reference pre-dates the beginnings of official colonisation of the country, though. On Thursday, 20 December 1832, the Reverend Henry Williams records in his diary that "the weather is fine. Turned the boys out to play at cricket by way of a finish and to prepare them for operations in the morning. Very expert, good bowlers." A few entries later we read that "the boys practised on Horotutu Beach at 2 p.m. near Paihia"[7] which is near Waitangi on the northern tip of the North Island. Three years later, Charles Darwin refers to Maoris playing cricket over Christmas at Waitate.

The second quarter of the century was the period in which

Visiting Australian and Philadelphian cricket teams, c.1884. The Americans have
since lost interest in cricket while the Australians have taken too much

the colonisation of New Zealand, Australia and Canada went into high gear. Australia had been developed partly as a penal colony, but by the middle of the century it was clear that all three lands were going to be populated by British emigrants, and that they would become important constituent parts of the British Empire. India and South Africa presented different situations: India was already very heavily populated by an advanced culture, so their inclusion into the Empire was by conquest of the indigenous people rather than by just turning up and claiming the empty spaces for queen and country; while Southern Africa was the subject of a systematic rape by many different colonial powers. It was not until the beginning of the 20th century that British supremacy was firmly established there.

Cricket was not the only ball game the colonists took with them. Golf also travelled overseas, introduced into the states of Georgia and South Carolina in America at the end of the 18th century, and by the East India Company to Calcutta around 1830. There are also records of the game reaching Melbourne in the 1840s. Football was also played everywhere that the great British colonists went, although it was still little more than an undisciplined kicking game. The sports which the colonials most indulged in were, needless to say, the field sports of hunting, shooting and fishing, which had the added appeal of exotic game to pursue. Hunting tigers in the Indian jungle from the back of an elephant was far more thrilling than chasing a fox across the Leicestershire countryside on the back of even the best steeplechaser.

George III was on the throne when the revolutionary war resulted in the independence of the United States. It also resulted in a Darwinian change to the sports played in America: they adapted to the native environment over the years, changing rounders into baseball and football into American football, as well as creating brand new games like basketball. Only golf, which was reintroduced in the 19th century, and the post-revolutionary sport of lawn tennis ever really took root in America from Britain. Both are intrinsically individual sports rather than team sports. Does the post-revolutionary American psyche prefer self-reliance to depending on others? Did the wide open spaces of the American plains breed a man who has gotta do what a man's gotta do, rather than a man who's gotta do what his team-mates want him to do?

George III's son, the Prince Regent, later George IV, added his own footnote to the development of team sports, although his influence was far from direct. Like his grandfather, he enjoyed gambling, and thus his main sporting interests were in horse-racing and boxing. He lost vast sums of money on the turf, bringing himself and the monarchy into even more disrepute than his mad father and his own treatment of his wife and mistresses had already done, and he was equally incapable of picking the winner when it came to the ring. Such was the baleful influence of the Prince Regent, in many ways a man far more deserving of the guillotine than his hapless and distant cousin on the other side of the Channel, that cricket, in particular, made some efforts to shake off the influence of the gamblers and put its house in order. The formation of the Marylebone Cricket Club in 1787 meant that for the first time a ball game would be played regularly in London rather than in the countryside around the capital, and we see from about this time a much smaller business in wagering on cricket, which to begin with resulted in no small loss of popularity for the game. It would be quite wrong to suggest that the founders of the MCC took the moral high ground and tried to establish a club free of the evils of gambling; that was not their purpose and it is not what happened. It is only with hindsight two hundred years on that we can say that the two trends are connected, or at least synchronous. Whether the MCC hierarchy specifically helped to eliminate the worst of the gambling on cricket in its early years is at best open to debate. More likely, it happened despite the MCC's attitudes rather than because of them.

The French Revolution, from the storming of the Bastille in 1789 through the years of the Terror and into Napoleonic times, had one immediate effect and several longer term effects on the development of ball games on the English side of the Channel. To an extent, the causes of the revolution were related to sport. As Trevelyan pointed out, in England "squire, farmer, blacksmith and labourer, with their women and children came to see the fun, were at ease together and happy all the summer afternoon. If the French noblesse had been capable of playing cricket with their peasants, their chateaux would never have been burnt."[6]

The immediate effect of the original Bastille Day was the cancellation of the first-ever overseas cricket tour. The third Duke of Dorset, a noted patron of cricket, had been appointed Ambassador and Plenipotentiary at the Court of Louis XVI in 1784, and in May 1786, *The Times* carried a report with the dateline, Paris, 16 April:

"On Monday last, a cricket match was played by some English Gentlemen, in the Champs Elyses [sic]. His Grace of Dorset was, as usual, the most distinguished for skill and activity."

In 1789 (two years after the foundation of the Marylebone Cricket Club), the Duke arranged for a team of English cricketers to come to France to play an exhibition match against his own team. The touring team, which included the Earl of

Tankerville, got as far as Dover, but at this point they were intercepted by emissaries from Paris who told them of the outbreak of the revolution; and so the tour was cancelled. This was the first, but unfortunately not the last, cricket tour to be cancelled for political reasons.

The longer term effect of the French Revolution on the development of sport in Britain was a gradual democratisation of many English sports, and in the first few years of the 19th century a definite drop in the general popularity of the two more obviously privileged ball games of the time: cricket and golf. It is not possible to state clear cause and effect, as people did not put away their golf clubs or their cricket bats with a shrug of their aristocratic shoulders or a bloodthirsty shout of "*Vive la revolution*". They just did not play as often. Certainly in Edinburgh, for example, there were many cases of members of the Honourable Company of Edinburgh golfers being attacked or abused on the golf course as well as in the streets of the city, which was quite an incentive not to carry on playing, or parading the Silver Club through the streets of St Andrews. All across Scotland, golfers were put off playing by the threat of being singled out as targets for class hatred, with the result that golf courses began to fall into disrepair. In England, where the aristocratic press, government and opinion-makers had been able to emphasise the bloodletting and the social evils of the French Revolution rather more than the benefits it brought to the ordinary French people, the anti-aristocratic feeling was held in better check, but still the Blackheath Golf Club, the oldest in England, felt the pinch, and not only because the club's large Scottish membership had dropped out.

Cricket was affected, too, even though it had played its part in the 18th century in uniting the different social classes. The formation of the Marylebone Cricket Club in 1787 had largely coincided with (and been a part cause of) the demise of cricket at Hambledon in Hampshire, but the new club's aristocratic founders did not create an organisation entirely in tune with the times. The MCC survived, but it was not a major power in its early years. Arthur Haygarth (1825–1903), who could claim the title of cricket's first statistician, published fourteen volumes of his *Cricket Scores and Biographies,* which list the scores of all major games played in the early years of the 19th century. He lists thirty-three matches in 1798, but from 1801 to 1817, he finds no more than fourteen games in any one year. In 1811 and 1812, he reports on just two matches each year.

Neither of these two matches were that archetypically class fixture, Gentlemen versus Players, although the first game in this series had taken place in July 1806. The Gentlemen were the amateurs, the wealthy who played cricket for the pure pleasure it brought them, not to mention the gambling profits. The Players were the professional cricketers, employed by the amateurs to bowl at them for hours on end. The second game in the series took place in 1819, four years after the defeat of Napoleon at Waterloo, an event which proved to all and sundry that the English way of doing things was obviously best. Quite probably, the English self-confidence which allowed this small island nation to rule the world for a hundred years all stems from this Belgian battle, so the spread of English sports around the world can be seen to be a direct result of the Duke of Wellington's victory. He, of course, famously said that the Battle of Waterloo was won on the playing fields of Eton – where, at the time, there were no rules of fair play.

When the Gentlemen met the Players on the cricket field, it was easy to tell which was which. The amateur Gentlemen looked elegant, moved languidly and being natural officer material, produced the best leadership, the best tactics and the most exciting strokeplay. Unfortunately, they were not as good at the game as the Players. The Players, on the other hand, were professional cricketers employed to do very little except play the game. They were artisans with no more say in their destinies than the workers in the cotton factories of Lancashire, but they were able to earn a living from their sporting prowess. As a general rule, the Gentlemen batted and the Players bowled. Cricket always was a batsman's game, but it was the bowlers who won the matches. Over the years of the fixture, the professional Players won far more often than the amateur Gentlemen, because they bowled better.

Cricket was not the only sport which yielded professional players: horse-racing, boxing and golf all had full-time, paid participants at this time, but none of them were paid very much. If they wanted to earn good money, they had to get involved in the betting, either by putting their own money on their own chances of victory, or, equally commonly, by selling their success to the highest bidder. There was no real incentive for a working-class man to consider a career as a sportsman, because there was not much extra money available, little glory and no future if injury cut the career short or even if it was left to the natural ageing processes to throw the sporting hero on the scrapheap. The only advantage was in the working conditions. Cricket pitches, golf courses, race tracks and even the prize ring were preferable to the dark satanic mills of the early years of the Industrial Revolution. The working hours were shorter, too.

The success of British industry in the 19th century meant that the owners of the factories needed all the workers they could get, and wanted to keep for themselves as much of the

Supporters leaving the ground after a Notts County game, 1901. Once legislation freed up Saturday afternoons for many workers, football attendances rocketed

profit as they could get. So the working population of England found themselves undertaking exhaustingly long hours of back-breaking work, and when those long hours were over they went back to the insanitary hovels where they had to live. That gave them very little free time to watch other men play sport, and even less energy to take part themselves. Until the Factory Act of 1833 and the Ten Hours Bill of 1847, there was no respite for working men, not to mention working women and children who were even more exploited because they did not have to be paid as much. The idea of a free Saturday afternoon did not gain general acceptance until a further act, in 1863, and even then many industries ignored it. It was thus inevitable that the organisation and development of our national sports should be left to the Gentlemen of the age, even though the advances in tactics and skill were almost entirely achieved by the Players.

By the middle of the 19th century, though, the line between Gentlemen and Players, off the cricket field at least, was beginning to blur. The Corn Laws were repealed in 1845, representing a victory for the new industrialists over the landed aristocracy, and from this time, the pendulum swung slowly away from the old established order. Industrialists made wealthy by their factories were able to spend their money in a way that the landed gentry no longer could. Machines brought profits which were liquid assets, able to be spent however their owner wished to spend them. Land did not create cash, so although the noblemen with their vast estates could stage horse races or cricket matches on their land, they were not always in a position to finance outside events, and still less to gamble on them.

The new industrialists did not always turn to sport. Many thought that cultural awareness was what they needed to prove their worth in society, not sporting connections. Culture meant architecture (a rash of ugly Victorian piles sprang up all across the country as a result of well-meant but entirely tasteless benefactions), it meant music, it meant painting and it meant the theatre. It is a remarkable testimony to the way these people spent their wealth that British music, architecture and theatre in the first two-thirds of the 19th century were almost at their nadir. It was only in literature, in novels and poetry, that England went through a golden age, and these were arts which did not attract industrial sponsorship.

Sport fared better from the new money, because there was no pretension to it. Racing was the sport of kings, and kings were a little out of fashion with the *nouveau riche,* so the money began to flow into other areas. The new industrialists were trying to be philanthropists, too, and liked to think they had the welfare of their workers at heart. Anything that working men could enjoy – always providing that their enjoyment did not detract from their obligation to put in a full day's work six days a week – was a worthy place to put some of their wealth.

Outdoor team games were not the only ones that attracted the attention and the interest of Victorian gentlemen and would-be gentlemen. Croquet, bowls, hockey, cycling, swimming and rowing all began to be organised in the first years of Victoria's reign. The world's first swimming baths opened in Liverpool in 1828. The first Oxford v Cambridge boat race took place in 1829, and ten years later, the first regatta at Henley took place. Kirkpatrick Macmillan, a Dumfries blacksmith, developed his pedal bicycle in 1839, and the Blackheath Hockey Club was formed around 1840, the first hockey club in Britain (it is not clear who they played against until the formation of the second hockey club in Britain, which was probably the Teddington club on the other side of London). In 1849 W.W. Mitchell, a Glasgow solicitor, was given the task of codifying the rules of bowls.

The key element in all these developments was competition. The growth of industry had shown the virtues of a competitive economy, and all the new leaders of industry were by definition believers in the merits of competition. Fair competition was perhaps a different concept altogether, but on the sports field, the excitement for these new sporting benefactors was in the competition, not in the absolute values of technical skill or the beauty of the game. Theirs was not a Regency-style lust for gambling nor a simple devotion to the purity of physical exercise. They just liked to win.

Organising and sponsoring sporting fixtures also allowed these industrialists to control their lives, and the lives of others, in play as much as in work. The same techniques that had stood them in good stead in their capitalist working lives would serve them in their leisure hours, and they would use the same modern inventions to challenge the traditions of sport and indeed, of all aspects of their lives. So the railway network, which by 1847 already extended over ten thousand miles of track, became an essential tool in expanding sports around the country, as people and teams searched ever farther to find worthy opposition. The postal systems, revitalised by the introduction of the penny post in 1840, were used to build sporting relationships with distant competitors, and the newspapers soon saw the advantages, in terms of increased readership, of reporting scores and results of the leading fixtures of the day. Sports were becoming an industry in themselves, a profitable extra for the owners of the fledgling communications systems in Britain and elsewhere. Sport was turning professional, whether the establishment wanted it or not.

Professional occupations need somebody to pay the money that keeps them going, and in the case of Victorian sport, it was the spectator as much as the sponsor who paid. The increase in leisure time that came as a result of the various Factory Acts of the latter part of the century meant that the working people were looking for ways to spend their newly won money in their newly won free time. For some, participating in sport was the perfect answer, but for the majority, who did not have the skills to take part, watching the experts play became a compulsive pastime. The rise of the spectator was a necessary element in the rise of professional sport, although it sometimes seems as though sport a century or so later can do without any spectators apart from the audience beyond the television lens. Without the desire and the opportunity for the masses to watch sports, all the regimentation on the sports pitches of all the public schools in Britain would have made no difference. People loved the short-term excitement of professional sport. They loved the fact that it was something they could understand if not control, an area of their otherwise undistinguished lives in which they could, for ninety minutes or so, be experts and live beyond their humdrum and dirty existences through the skills of others. Sport took people out of their own lives and into a life somewhere between dreams and reality, a life where your hopes could be pinned to the striped shirts of a football team for a short while, and where happiness could be found, albeit briefly, in the collective enthusiasm of the crowds on the terraces. (All the above, of course, rarely applied to supporters of Stoke City, who never gave their fans much to pin their hopes to.) Sport is, in the words of Derek Birley, "a dream world offering escape from harsh reality and the disturbing prospect of change".[9] People will pay for that.

The morality of Victorian life was built on the twin tenets of Empire and Industry. The two were intertwined and interdependent: the conquest of Empire gave the raw materials for the growth of Industry and the growth of Industry gave the British the means to reach, conquer and communicate with their Empire. The Victorians' supreme organisational skills, which allowed them to invent the processes and run the factories in Britain to create her industrial strength, as well as to rule in places as far apart as New Zealand, Hong Kong and Jamaica, also led them towards the organisation of those unruly and corrupt sports that until then, despite the best efforts of Frederick, Prince of Wales and others, had remained the birthright of the common people of Britain. What the effete Hanoverian society could not do the more vigorous and practical Victorians did with ease: they took hold of these violent and spontaneous pastimes and turned them with ruthless energy into violent but highly organised sports, with all the right moral overtones of spiritual welfare and physical improvement. They tried to steal them away from the working classes, but at least in the case of association football and professional rugby league, they never quite succeeded. So organised sports in Victorian England became the sublimated outlet for all the excess organising energy of the ruling classes, who bowdlerised the games but at the same time turned them into perhaps the most popular of all Victorian inventions. They were eventually to become the first major items of world culture, losing a little of their Britishness as they did so, but they remain as permanent a memorial to Victorian inventiveness as any of Brunel's bridges or Darwin's theories or Dickens' novels.

"PITCHES A WICKET, PLAYS AT CRICKET"

There is absolutely no agreement whatsoever by the experts on how cricket began. Perhaps it was in Northern Europe, perhaps in mediaeval England. The Northern Europe theory stems from what the eccentric but nevertheless brilliant Rowland Bowen called "the first certain reference to cricket anywhere"[1], which is in St Omer, in northern France, in 1478. The reference is to "criquet" but Bowen was convinced that the reading of the word could not possibly be open to doubt. He discovered that in that part of what had been the lands of the House of Burgundy, a Celtic tribe, the Atrebates, once lived, who had a numbering system based on eleven; so the logic of an eleven-a-side game developing from that culture seemed incontestable. He even found a Roman noble based in Gaul in the 5th-century AD, by the name of Apollinaris Sidonius, who played a ball game which to Bowen ought to have been cricket or its fore-runner, even if Sidonius never gave it a name. Unfortunately, the Visigoths wiped out all trace of his cricket pitches, so we have no proof of what he played. More recent cricket historians seem to regard Bowen's ideas as little more than hypothesis, but there is no absolute proof that his theory is wrong. Some radicals even propose Scotland as the birthplace of this essentially

English game, but most historians believe that it began on the Weald of southern England, in the counties of Kent, Surrey and Sussex, as a pastime for shepherds who had little else to do while tending their sheep. What we do know is that the Hambledon club in Hampshire in the 1750s became the first organised centre of cricket, a tiny village club that became strong enough for a few short years to challenge and beat any club that came up against it.

The main instigators of the success of the Hambledon club were a clergyman, the Reverend Charles Powlett, a publican, Richard Nyren, and a local squire, Philip Dehany. Powlett was a son of the third Duke of Bolton. He was born in 1728, and was educated at Westminster School and Trinity College, Cambridge. He gained his MA in 1755, at the age of twenty-seven, and was appointed curate of Itchen Abbas, not far from Hambledon, in 1763, by which time he was thirty-five years old. Clearly, he was not a man who did things swiftly. He remained curate there for twenty-two years, never looking as though he would make any move up through the ranks of the clergy, perhaps because the local bishop had noticed Powlett's complete lack of spiritual qualities which shines through all descriptions of his life. Still, he was no doubt quite happy at Itchen Abbas, and only moved to become Rector of St Martin's, near Looe in Cornwall, when he was nearing sixty years old.

H.S. Altham[2] states that Powlett was the son of the third Duke of Bolton and Lavinia Fenton, the Duke having done what many scions of noble houses have done over the years and become involved with a leading performer from the London stage. Lavinia, Duchess of Bolton was the singer who created the role of Polly Peachum in John Gay's biggest success, "The Beggar's Opera", which was first performed in 1728. In the play,

Polly marries the villainous Macheath (Mack the Knife in the Brecht/Weill version two centuries later), but in real life Miss Fenton's marriage was much happier if no longer lasting. It was certainly not long-lasting enough for the Reverend Charles to have been a legitimate son, as Lavinia did not marry the Duke of Bolton until 1751, by which time Charles was already almost twenty-three years old, and Lavinia was forty-three. Lavinia gave birth to Charles in the same year that she opened at Lincoln's Inn Fields in the biggest success of her career, a success which meant she was paid the enormous salary of thirty shillings a week. In return, she had to perform the opera sixty-two times during that season, beginning on 29 January 1728. The third Duke of Bolton saw her performance as Polly Peachum on the opening night, and fell in love with her when she sang, "Oh ponder well! Be not severe." That they did not marry for over two decades may be because Lavinia took to heart the words delivered by Polly Peachum's father: "Do you think your mother and I should have lived comfortably so long together if ever we had been married?" Lavinia lived only nine years as Duchess of Bolton, having been the Duke's mistress for well over twice as long. However, the connection between the Boltons and the Fentons continues to this day. The dukedom of Bolton died out in the 1790s, but at the same time a barony was created. In 1991, Richard Orde-Powlett, the seventh Baron Bolton, married another Lavinia Fenton, two hundred and forty years after his ancestor had done exactly the same thing.

Powlett, being born out of wedlock, was thus denied the courtesy title "honourable", and seems to have qualified for the title of bastard by character as well as by birth. Philip Dehany (1733–1809), a man of similar moral outlook, was an acquaintance of Powlett's from Westminster days, and subsequently the

Richard Nyren's Bat and Ball Inn overlooking Broadhalfpenny Down.
Pen drawing from W. W. Reade's *Annals of Cricket*, 1896

squire of Kempshott Park, not far away from Hambledon. The
two of them appear to have helped the Hambledon Cricket
Club to grow to its position of eminence not particularly
through any love of cricket, nor even to bask in the reflected
glory of the local sportsmen, but because it gave them a wonderful medium for their love of gambling. This was Powlett and
Dehany's driving urge which made the growth of cricket at
Hambledon possible, but it is Richard Nyren who is remembered as the central figure of cricket on Broadhalfpenny Down,
a bleak heath in the middle of nowhere, two miles outside the
village of Hambledon. Nyren's uncle was one Richard Newland,
a surgeon who had been the star player for the Duke of Dorset's
team at Slindon in Sussex a generation earlier. Nyren was, until
1771, the landlord of the Bat and Ball Inn overlooking
Broadhalfpenny Down, which still operates as a pub (and crick-

et museum) today. Then he moved two miles down the road into the village of Hambledon and took over as landlord of the George Inn, but still played regularly for Hambledon. Powlett, Nyren and Dehany formed their cricket club some time in the late 1760s, and by the mid 1770s, their team was the strongest in England. Its immortality, however, owes as much to the book written by Richard Nyren's son John, *The Young Cricketer's Tutor*, published in 1833, as it does to the team's cricketing brilliance. The son proved a chronicler equal to the father's best efforts.

The names of the men who played for Hambledon have thus been handed down over two centuries, and they are the names of the first English team still remembered today. We know the names of a few individual sportsmen – jockeys, prize-fighters and gamblers – from earlier ages, but this is the first team we know of. Their names still evoke a long-lost golden age of bucolic summer days.

There was Richard Nyren, the captain, club secretary, treasurer, mine host and driving spirit and, "although a very stout man (standing about five foot nine)" he was a left-handed cricketer of brilliance. His son described him as "a good face-to-face unflinching, uncompromising, independent man", or what anybody but his son would have called "a stroppy bugger". "I never saw a finer specimen of the thoroughbred old English yeoman than Richard Nyren" – a man who clearly aroused the admiration of his son, and by his account, of all he met. Then there was Edward Aburrow, a shoemaker and unlike Nyren, a native of Hambledon. He was known to all as "Curry" for a reason that not even Nyren could remember. Aburrow was a safe and steady batter and "one of our best long fields". William Barber was the man who took over as landlord of the Bat and

Ball Inn from Nyren in 1771. He was a fine bowler, if not as fast as Nyren, nor as his relative by marriage Thomas Brett. Brett was a local farmer and John Nyren called him "beyond all comparison the fastest as well as the straightest bowler that was ever known". This was in the days of underarm bowling, at a wicket with no middle stump. The speed of his bowling can be assessed by the fact that many of his victims were stumped, by the great Thomas Sueter. Brett was obviously fast in his day, but one cannot remember the fast bowlers of this century, such as Curtly Ambrose or Dennis Lillee or Harold Larwood, getting many of their victims stumped, especially by a wicketkeeper wearing neither pads nor gloves.

Thomas Sueter, another local man, was described thus: "What a handful of steel-hearted soldiers are in an important pass, such was Tom in keeping the wicket." He was also "one of the manliest and most graceful of hitters", and was one of the first players to dare to leave his crease to hit the ball; "and egad! it went as if it had been fired", according to young John. In case you feel that his qualities on the cricket field are enough to distinguish him as a man amongst men, we also learn that Sueter was of "so amiable disposition that he was the pet of all the neighbourhood; so honourable a heart that his word was never questioned" and, just to make him entirely hateful, he was a remarkably handsome man, about five foot ten tall. Oh, and he had a fine tenor singing voice, with which he could have made his fortune. We are beginning to understand that John Nyren looked at his father's team-mates through utterly uncritical eyes, but that is why they live on: they were not half-hearted heroes, they were a boy's whole world.

The names of the rest make for happy reading: William Hogsflesh, a bowler, "Little George" Leer, "our best long-stop", and "Buck, whose real name was Peter Steward". Actually, it appears his real name was Peter Stewart, but as everybody called him Buck, it did not really matter. As the Reverend Mr Reynell Cotton of Winchester wrote in his song "Cricket":

> Buck, Curry and Hogsflesh, and Barber and Brett,
> Whose swiftness in bowling was ne'er equalled yet;
> I had almost forgot, they deserve a large bumper;
> Little George the long-stop, and Tom Sueter, the stumper.

It seems unlikely from that brief quatrain that the Reverend Mr Cotton was ever able to give up his day job. But the two most important players after Richard Nyren were none of these. They were John Small the Elder and Thomas Taylor.

John Small was originally a gamekeeper and, with Nyren, about ten years older than most of the other Hambledon players. He was a fine mid-wicket fielder and as a batsman "a star in the first magnitude". In 1775, Small and Nyren were the central characters in a drama that almost wrecked the Hambledon Club, and which showed how important gambling was to the popularity of cricket. Hambledon were playing Surrey on Broadhalfpenny Down over four days in July 1775, and were in trouble in their second innings. With five wickets down for few runs, the gamblers beyond the boundary were doing everything they could to lay off any bets they had on Hambledon, and put big sums, even at short odds, on Surrey. John Small was still not out, but when Richard Nyren came out to the wicket to join him, all was apparently lost. But no, thanks to a brilliant display of batting, including 136 not out by Small and 98 from Nyren (his highest score ever for Hambledon – so near and yet so far), Hambledon emerged the winners. Yet when he was out, Nyren was accosted by a couple of gamblers who, far from congratulating him on his efforts, told him in no uncertain terms how much money his batting had cost them. The gamblers were no casual spectators, either. They were Reverend Charles Powlett, chief patron of the club and curate of Itchen Abbas, and his close friend Philip Dehany. Nyren, who as we have noted was not afraid to express his opinion "face-to-face unflinching", told the two gentlemen that he was glad they had lost money and advised them in future not to bet against Hambledon. One can imagine that the atmosphere at the next few committee meetings was strained.

John Small the Elder was also a musician, and enjoyed playing the double bass. On one occasion, also in 1775, the Duke of Dorset was so grateful to Small for his efforts in helping Hambledon win a game that many thought lost (thus giving His Grace a return on his gambling investment that he had also thought lost) that he sent Small a violin, and paid the carriage. Small returned the compliment "like a true and simple-hearted Englishman" by sending the Duke two bats and two balls from his workshop in Dragon Street, Petersfield, and paid the carriage. Outside Small's workshop there was a sign which read:

> Here lives John Small
> Makes bats and balls,
> Pitches a wicket, plays at cricket
> With any man in England.

The rhyme and scansion of this little poem makes one wonder whether the Reverend Mr Cotton of Winchester was involved in its composition.

The game which encouraged this exchange of gifts was played on 22 May 1775 at the Artillery Ground in London (where, like Broadhalfpenny Down, cricket is still played) between Five of All England and Five of Hambledon. It was

Cricket played as it was in the Artillery Ground, London, 1785

during this march that the famous Edward "Lumpy" Stevens, possibly the greatest bowler of the 18th century, bowled so straight at Small that three times the ball passed between the two stumps and underneath the one bail without disturbing the wicket. John Nyren records that under the 1744 laws which applied then, Small was clearly not out, but "it was considered to be a hard thing upon the bowler that his straightest balls should be thus sacrificed". Within about five years, a middle stump had become part of the wicket, thanks mainly to the luck of John Small the Elder.

Tom Taylor was another Hambledonian who helped to change the laws of cricket. Taylor was "a short well-made man" whose particular strength was in his fielding. Many unwary batsman were run out by the speed of Taylor's returns as they cantered what looked like a safe single. As a batsman, he loved to cut the ball. As any batsman will tell you, it is difficult to cut every ball, especially the straight ones. In order to prevent the uncuttable straight ones from hitting his wicket (even though there was a chance the ball might go straight through as it did with John Small), Taylor developed a technique of putting his leg in the way. Although this must have hurt in those days before the invention of pads, it at least meant he was not out. It was not cricket in the way that John Nyren described his Hambledon heroes as playing the game, but it worked; it also led to the introduction of the leg before wicket law in 1774.

In those days, the laws of cricket were agreed and amended from time to time by an ad hoc group of cricket-loving gentlemen. They got together when an issue – such as the leg before wicket problem – needed to be resolved, so that disputes would be kept to a minimum. Among the gentlemen who were present at the Star and Garter in Pall Mall when the laws were revised on 25 February 1774 were the Reverend Charles Powlett and Philip Dehany of the Hambledon Club, as well as the Duke of Dorset, the Earl Tankerville and Sir Horace Mann, who were to play a leading role in the formation of the Marylebone Cricket Club three years later. "Silver Billy" Beldham (1766–1862), the best batsman of his generation, wrote that the lbw law was not wanted until "one of our best hitters was shabby enough to get his leg in the way and take advantage of the bowlers, and when Tom Taylor did the same, the bowlers found themselves beaten and the law was passed". The motivation for the change in the law was not to eliminate "shabby" batting, but to eliminate disputes over the way the game was played. Disputes over the way the game was played brought far more serious disputes about the honouring of gambling debts.

By this time, too, bowling, though still underarm, was not delivered all along the ground nor as a full toss. It pitched once, and often turned, cut or spun off the wicket. As a result, cricket bats could no longer be curved sticks more like a hockey stick or a shepherd's crook, as you could not hit the ball any longer with a bat like that. The cricket bats had originally been designed more for defending the wicket than attacking the bowling, and thus looked like slightly curved clubs. The wickets in the early days were only a few inches high but originally up to six feet wide, and the ball was rolled along the ground. Once the ball started bouncing, the effect on the game was revolutionary. The bats were no longer suitable for scoring runs, but the wickets were also too low to be hit with any regularity. So the wickets grew taller and narrower, and the bats had to change shape to even up the battle once more.

They gradually became straight, flat-faced pieces of willow like the bats of today. This led one more pioneer of gamesmanship to test the laws to their utmost and give the Star and Carter law-makers a little more to think about. Thomas "Shock" White of Reigate came out to bat for Surrey against Hambledon on 23 September 1771 with a bat wider than the wicket, precipitating a law on the maximum width of bats. We do not know how many runs White scored with his mega-bat, but we do know that Hambledon, using ordinary bats, won by just one run in the end. In 1774 it was decreed for the first time that bats could be no wider than four and a quarter inches, or less than half the nine-inch width of the wicket. It was not until 1835 that the maximum length of a bat was fixed at thirty-eight inches. White was a great batsman of his time, one of the few to match the great John Small, and scarcely needed a bat as wide as he used on that fateful afternoon. In July of the same year,

Four Surrey Cricketers: Tom Sherman, Julius Caesar, William Caffyn
and Tom Lockyer. Lithograph after J.C. Anderson, 1852

using a bat of reasonable proportions, White had scored 197
runs in two innings for Surrey and Kent against Middlesex and
Hampshire, a huge total for the time.

Cricket has always been considered a batsman's game, and
it has always been the professionals who have been asked to do
the boring bit, the bowling. If you do something every day and
get paid for it, the chances are that you will become quite good
at it. Thus it was that the skills of the professional bowlers,
Edward "Lumpy" Stevens, Thomas Brett and the like, forced
the batsmen to stretch the rules as far as they could to wrest the

advantage back. The legislators, on the other hand, generally found in favour of the bowlers and the gamblers, forcing through the lbw law, and the regulations about bat sizes and the number of stumps. But the biggest battle was still to come, the battle about "round-arm" bowling.

David Harris was the forerunner of this style of bowling, although he never employed it himself. Another Hambledon man, he was, in John Nyren's eyes at least, a man of the utmost integrity, so he fitted in well with all his Hambledon team-mates. He was also the fastest bowler that had ever been seen. He bowled the ball from the height of his armpit, making it bounce almost as much as an overarm ball today, but such was his accuracy that he was reputed to wear the grass out where the ball pitched over after over. The speed of his deliveries broke many fingers, and his accuracy was such that very few runs were scored off his bowling. "Unless a batter were of the very first class," wrote Nyren, "and accustomed to the best style of stop-ping, he could do little or nothing with Harris." Suddenly, cricket threatened once again to become a bowler's game, so the batsmen had to develop "the best style of stopping". One of the first requirements of any batsman wanting to stop Harris was a good bat. Although as a result of Shock White's antics in 1771, there was a maximum width laid down for the bat, it was the problems that David Harris presented which led to the devel-opment of the most practical shape of cricket bat – the relative proportions of handle and blade, the weight and so on. Straight bowling required a straight bat and straight defence, all funda-mentals of the art of batting today. The bounce of the ball also led to pleas (from David Harris as much as from anybody else) to raise the height of the stumps, which happened in 1788. By the time Harris retired from the game at the end of the century, the game was looking much more like the game we know today than it had when he burst on to the scene in 1778.

Harris was only forty-eight years old when he died, and in his latter years he was a martyr to gout. Although he was of absolutely no use in the field, such was his skill as a bowler, that even when crippled by gout he would make his way to the ground on crutches, and then sit in an armchair placed for him at the bowler's end, where he could sit between deliveries. We have no idea what happened if the batsman hit the ball back at Harris causing it to cannon off the chair. These days it would count as five runs to the batting side, but as Harris was such an accurate bowler, perhaps nobody ever presumed to try to hit the ball straight and hard back at him.

One aspect of the game that has changed very much since the days of David Harris is the quality of the wicket itself. In the late 18th century, the side that won the toss had the right to choose where the wickets would be pitched. There was no carefully prepared flat wicket, put together by a professional groundsman, to give equal opportunity to batsman and bowler – although, come to think of it, that does not always happen two hundred years later, either. At Hambledon it was the habit of Richard Nyren to allow David Harris the right to decide where the wicket should be pitched whenever Hambledon won the toss. John Nyren reports that Harris was particularly skilful at this, always trying to choose a strip of turf that would suit the entire side, not just himself. Of course, as the best bowler in the side, any strip that suited him would suit the whole team, but we are led to believe that Harris was far more noble in his choice than his main rival as champion bowler of the day, Lumpy Stevens. Lumpy always looked for a strip that would ensure that he would take more wickets than anybody else, while Harris

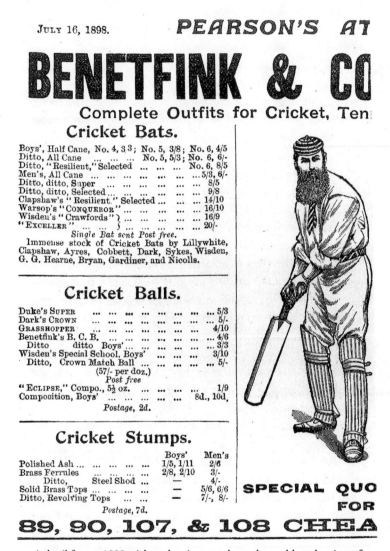

PEARSON'S AT

BENETFINK & CO

Complete Outfits for Cricket, Ten

Cricket Bats.

Boys', Half Cane, No. 4, 3 3 ; No. 5, 3/8 ; No. 6, 4/5
Ditto, All Cane ... ... No. 5, 5/3 ; No. 6, 6/-
Ditto, "Resilient," Selected ... ... No. 6, 8/5
Men's, All Cane 5/3, 6/-
Ditto, ditto, Super 8/5
Ditto, ditto, Selected 9/8
Clapshaw's "Resilient." Selected 14/10
Warsop's "CONQUEROR" 16/10
Wisden's "Crawfords" ⎰ 16/9
"EXCELLER" ... ... ⎱ 20/-
Single Bat sent Post free.
Immense stock of Cricket Bats by Lillywhite,
Clapshaw, Ayres, Cobbett, Dark, Sykes, Wisden,
G. G. Hearne, Bryan, Gardiner, and Nicolls.

Cricket Balls.

Duke's SUPER ... ... ••• ... ... ••• ... 5/3
Dark's CROWN ... ••• ••• 5/-
GRASSHOPPER ... ••• ... ... ••• 4/10
Benetfink's B. C. B. ... ... •• 4/6
Ditto ditto Boys'... ... ... 3/3
Wisden's Special School, Boys' ... ... ••• 3/10
Ditto, Crown Match Ball ... ... ••• ... ••• 5/-
(57/- per doz.)
Post free
"ECLIPSE," Compo., 5½ oz. ... ••• 1/9
Composition, Boys' ... ... 8d., 10d.
Postage, 2d.

Cricket Stumps.

	Boys'	Men's
Polished Ash	1/5, 1/11	2/6
Brass Ferrules	2/8, 2/10	3/-
Ditto, Steel Shod ...	—	4/-
Solid Brass Tops	—	5/6, 6/6
Ditto, Revolving Tops	—	7/-, 8/-

Postage, 7d.

SPECIAL QUO

FOR

89, 90, 107, & 108 CHEA

A detail from a 1898 cricket advertisement shows the wealth and variety of
equipment already available, including one W. Lillywhite's early products

just looked for a strip that would ensure that Hambledon scored more than their opponents.

What Harris usually decided on was a wicket on slightly rising ground, which meant that he could pitch the ball on a very gentle slope so that it came at the batsman fast and rising. The result was that Harris took many more wickets by catches than his contemporaries. Despite the increase in size of the stumps, he relied on the catching skills of his colleagues to dismiss the batsmen, and in that tactic too, foreshadowed the professional game of a century later and more.

In 1792, seven years after the Reverend Charles Powlett had moved to Cornwall and the last year in which cricket was played on Broadhalfpenny Down for over a century, Tom Walker, another great Hambledon batsman, decided to have a go at bowling. He was their opening batsman, a great if slow accumulator of runs, and was scarcely ever invited to bowl. Perhaps because he was just no good at it, perhaps because he was generally regarded as an uncoordinated stringy bag of bones who could not work out where his arms ought to be when he bowled, or perhaps because he was a canny thinker about the game, he bowled round arm, with his arm level with his shoulder as he bowled. Nyren was shocked, and the club quickly imposed a ban on such bowling in future. But the seeds had been sown.

A quarter of a century later, John Willes (1778–1852) of Headcorn in Kent took up Tom Walker's style of bowling, and this time the authorities took notice of the new technique. What followed was a long struggle to legitimise round-arm bowling, which was ultimately successful but which along the way put paid to the career of Willes. Legend has it that John Willes and his sister Christina between them invented overarm

Lord's cricket ground in 1837.
Detail from a design printed on a silk handkerchief

bowling in the early years of the 19th century, mainly because
Christina could not bowl underarm with her vast skirts and
crinoline as she played in the family garden near Maidstone.
Her brother realised that the way she was forced to bowl made
her a far more formidable opponent, and he resolved to try out
her method for himself.

His first match at Lord's was for the Gentlemen against the
Players on 7, 8 and 9 July 1806, but we do not know whether
he dared to bowl in the round-arm style in that game. Among
his fellow Gentlemen was the Reverend Lord Frederick
Beauclerk, like Charles Powlett a less than reverend man of the

cloth and a descendant of noble extramarital affairs, in his case the one between Charles II and Nell Gwyn. He was perhaps the most powerful personality in cricket in the late Georgian era, and it was said that he only objected to round-arm bowling when it was employed against him, but never when John Willes was on his side. By 1807, Willes was using this new method quite regularly in games in Kent, and was not always told it was unfair. In that year, he played for XIII of Kent against XIII of England, and the *Kentish Gazette* reported that "straight-armed bowling, introduced by John Willes Esq., was generally practised in this game, and proved a great obstacle against getting runs in comparison to what might have been got by straight-forward bowling". For the next fifteen years, Willes bowled round arm whenever he could get away with it, even though he was often banned from playing and occasionally provoked such uproar that the match had to be abandoned. But he was a good cricketer (and that rarity, a gentleman, rather than a professional, who bowled) so he was able to carry on playing until he met his cricketing end at Lord's in 1822, when he was already forty-four years old, so quite probably ready to retire anyway. On 15 July that year he was no-balled for throwing when playing for Kent against MCC, and was so upset that he threw down the ball, climbed on to his horse and rode away from cricket for the last time.

His case was taken up almost immediately by two very different men. There was William Lillywhite, known as "The Nonpareil", whose first major game was in the year of Willes's final disgrace. Before Lillywhite retired and founded his sports shop, which still dominates Piccadilly Circus in London, he perfected the new system of round-arm bowling, and by 1827 he took part in three games for Sussex against All England, the first two of which Sussex won and the third of which was almost not played until the Sussex players agreed to "bowl fair, i.e. abstain from throwing". This final game was eventually won by All England, for whom the star was George Thomas Knight of Godmersham Park, near Ashford in Kent. Knight was the nephew of Jane Austen, who had lived not far from Hambledon for most of her life, and must have heard of the feats of the great cricketers of her day, even if she never saw them play. George Knight, though mainly a batsman, argued the cause of round-arm bowling very eloquently (and bowled it to great effect in that third match against Lillywhite's Sussex team), and despite the combined opposition of the likes of Thomas Lord, the man with the cricket ground in St John's Wood, and John Nyren, as well as many active cricketers of the day, by 1835, the law was changed.

One of the great opponents of the new bowling style was William Ward, who in 1820 had made 278 for MCC against Norfolk at Lord's, the first double century ever made in a major match, and the biggest score at cricket's headquarters for over a hundred years. On his debut at Lord's in 1810, he had made a duck. He, not surprisingly, did not agree with George Knight's argument that "batting dominates bowling to an extent detrimental to the game". Cricket always was a batsman's game, so anything that prevents the batsman from dominating cannot be good. Knight also pointed out that "to describe the new style as 'throwing' is nonsense; the straight arm is the very antithesis of a throw". In retrospect, we know he was right, but at the time, the change proposed was such a big one that the Marylebone Cricket Club, who had very quickly assumed control of the administration of cricket, was naturally very nervous.

One thing that Knight was entirely wrong about in arguing for round-arm bowling was that "it makes it impossible to bowl fast and dangerously". This argument was countered by William Denison, then only twenty-seven years old but later to become a noted writer on the game, who pointed out that it "cannot be faced on hard grounds, save at the most imminent peril". Denison was right, but the change was made and in the end it was the heirs of William Lillywhite who profited most from it. Sales of protective equipment for batsmen at their shop have continued profitably for a century and a half. Round-arm bowling was not overarm bowling, though. It was not until 1864 that overarm bowling was legalised.

The crucial game in the legalisation of overarm bowling was between Surrey County Cricket Club and the All-England Eleven on 26, 27 and 28 August 1862. There was bad feeling before the match even began, with many of the usual All-England players refusing to appear against a Surrey side which contained many players who had accepted terms to tour Australia which the All-England players had turned down as being too mean. All England batted first and very slowly compiled 503, finishing their innings at 5.30 on the second day. When Surrey batted, one of the opening bowlers was Edgar Willsher of Kent, who knew that umpire John Lillywhite considered his action overarm, and therefore illegal, and would no-ball him if ever he had the chance. But for the first two overs that Willsher bowled, Lillywhite did nothing. Then on the first ball of his third over, Lillywhite called no-ball, as he did with each of his next six deliveries. At this, Willsher hurled the ball away and stormed off the pitch, followed by the nine professionals in the England side. That left two batsmen, two umpires and two members of the fielding side, the amateurs Vyell Walker and the Hon. C.G. Lyttleton, on the pitch until eventually stumps were drawn for the day. This was sensational stuff, and it is hard with hindsight not to suspect both Willsher and Lillywhite of playing to the gallery, or at least to the committee rooms at Lord's, to make a point. Willsher apologised that evening to his good friend John Lillywhite for his behaviour, but Lillywhite carried on with his charade for the good of cricket. He said he would refuse to stand in any match where he could not enforce the law, even if many people did not agree with it (he quite probably being one of the many). So, in the spirit of pusillanimous expediency that was to become a regular feature of important sporting arguments down the years, Lillywhite was replaced by another umpire the next day. Willsher carried on bowling and the game petered out into a draw. With a speed of action that only MCC could achieve, the law was changed a mere six hundred and fifty-three days later, on 10 June 1864.

By the mid-1840s, cricket was very like the game we know today, overarm bowling always excepted, of course. The lawn mower was in the throes of invention, allowing groundsmen to prepare far more good wickets far more regularly than before. Much of the gambling had been eliminated with the rise of the Marylebone Cricket Club and the new Victorian morality, and the game was spreading its wings overseas. The success of the Hambledon club fifty years before and the general popularity of the games at Lord's and other grounds around the country showed anybody with a feel for commercial opportunities that there was not enough organised cricket to satisfy the public demand at the time. This was the Victorian age, though, and there were always opportunists willing to take advantage of the public tastes, and cricket proved to be no exception.

The first great cricket entrepreneur was William Clarke of Nottingham. He was born in 1798, but his great fame as a bowler did not come until he was in his late forties, even though he had played for the leading Nottinghamshire sides for years. In 1846, he hit upon the idea of forming a professional team, which he called the All-England Eleven, to play a series of games around the country against anybody who wished to oppose them. Their first game began on 31 August 1846, at the Hyde Park Ground in Sheffield, against a Sheffield XI, who proved that the odds were too great because they beat Clarke's XI by five wickets. This first game was played so late in the summer because Clarke had wanted to make sure that he could gather the eleven best players in the country, after their other cricket commitments had been completed for the year. Cricket generally finished early in August, to allow the gentlemen who ran the game within MCC to be on the moors in time for the Glorious Twelfth, which gave Clarke about a month of good cricketing time to fill.

He also decided that if the purpose of these games was to make money, he needed to take his team to the major towns where the ordinary people were starved of top-class cricket. This was the moment when cricket, the pastoral amateur game, set out on the road to becoming a professional urban sport. He followed up the defeat at Sheffield with two more games in Manchester and Leeds and finished the summer with a handsome profit. The next year, he organised ten fixtures, going as far north as Newcastle and Stockton on Tees, but never venturing further south than Birmingham. The authorities at Lord's looked rather sniffily at the entire project, but Clarke made a great deal of money. His players were greeted as heroes wherever they went, and by the third season, Clarke's All-England

William Clarke – the first great cricket entrepreneur.
Lithograph by John C. Anderson, 1852

Alfred Mynn – the Lion of Kent
Lithograph after J. C. Anderson

Eleven was the most profitable sporting organisation in Britain. As W.G. Grace was to recall in his autobiography, written in 1899, "a visit from the All-England team was a red-letter day wherever they went".[3]

There is an illustration owned by the Marylebone Cricket Club entitled "The England Eleven of 1847", showing rather perversely, fourteen men. Among them are several of the men whose business skills, rather than their cricketing talents, moved cricket rapidly into the professional age. There is "Parr", George

Parr of Nottingham who was the All-England Eleven's leading batsman and who took over as captain of the side when Clarke died in 1856; Mr A. Mynn, the highly paid amateur Alfred Mynn, the Lion of Kent and probably the greatest all-round cricketer of his generation; his fellow Kent player, the Norfolk-born Fuller Pilch; "Mr N. Felix", Nicholas Wanostrocht, known as Felix, whose *Felix on the Bat* published in 1845 was the first manual of cricketing technique; and Mr W. Denison, whom we have already met arguing with George Knight about the dangers of round-arm bowling but whose main claim to fame is that he became the first secretary of Surrey County Cricket Club. It was the establishment of the county cricket clubs that was to spell the end of the wandering England elevens in the 1860s, when a properly organised championship based on regional allegiances was recognised as the logical foundation for sporting competition.

Clarke's experiment of taking top-quality cricket to the urban masses was a huge success. It was the first real attempt to run a team sport as a business. Until Clarke took his revolutionary decision to form the All-England Eleven, cricket teams had been underwritten by rich sponsors and matches had been organised on an ad hoc basis between counties or town clubs, but as far as giving anybody a source of income was concerned, cricket was for gamblers, not businessmen. In 1840, there were probably not more than twenty professional cricketers in the country. There were plenty of men who were paid expenses when they played, or who were given employment by a wealthy sponsor so that they could turn out regularly for a particular side, but there were no more than a handful of full-time professional cricketers. By 1860, the number was nearer five hundred. These were men employed not only to play full time but

Evolution of Cricketing Dress
Pen drawings from W.W. Read's *Annals of Cricket*, 1896

also to coach at schools and universities and clubs around the country. A new industry was being born.

William Clarke's team travelled to Bristol in 1854 to play in a field behind the Full Moon Hotel, Stokes Croft, against XXII of West Gloucestershire. Among the many spectators that day was a six-year-old boy, there to watch the game with his mother. His father, Henry Mills Grace, organised the game and captained the local team, which also included the boy's eldest brother Henry and his Uncle Pocock. The boy was William Gilbert Grace, who would become the greatest cricketer of his age, possibly of all time, and by the end of the century perhaps the most famous Englishman in the world. The All-England Eleven won that day by 149 runs, despite the odds and the presence of two Graces, and came back to play again the following year. In 1855, another member of the family, Edward Mills Grace, aged fourteen, played and yet again the All-England Eleven won, this time by 165 runs. But the great William Clarke was so impressed by young Edward's fielding that he presented him with a bat. The torch was being passed on to the next generation – a generation that would take cricket to levels of skill, popularity and public passion that not even the astute Clarke could have imagined.

Clarke's only barrier to the long-term success of his team, and to his own personal wealth, was self-inflicted. His style of management and captaincy was overbearing and the professionals in his side did not all appreciate his wariness in monetary matters. He was mean in both his bowling and his financial dealings. Clarke took an amazing 2,385 wickets in seven seasons from 1847, when he was forty-nine years old, so he was well worth his place in his own team. In 1853, the year that Thomas Nixon – another Nottinghamshire cricketer – introduced cane-handled bats to make batting more comfortable if not easier, Clarke took 476 wickets, more than any bowler has ever taken in a Test career and half as many again as anybody has ever managed in a first-class season. However, by that year, there had been great discontent among his professional players, even though there was continuing and extravagant adulation among all the crowds they played for, and Clarke's great team began to crumble.

The second great cricket entrepreneur, John Wisden, broke away from Clarke at the end of 1852 and formed "The United Eleven", which also toured the cities of England doing good business. It had been early in September 1852 that many of the All-England Eleven, led by Wisden and his Sussex colleague James Dean, had signed a statement saying that they would never again play for any team controlled by Clarke, but there were many other cricketers eager to take their place, just as there were over a hundred years later when the Packer revolution scythed its way through the Test sides of the world. So for the next several seasons there were two national teams touring the country and making money for their backers. In 1862, this number was increased to three as a result of a dispute of a type that was to become endemic in Victorian sport and perhaps symbolic of the development of British society after the industrial revolution: North versus South. Many of the professionals in Wisden's United Eleven disproved the team name by disuniting and forming the separate "United South of England Eleven".

Wisden, a tiny man, is now best remembered for his *Cricketers' Almanack*, but his name was made first as a bowler who took all ten wickets in an innings clean bowled, the only man ever to do this in the history of the game. He achieved this amazing feat in the second innings of – wait for it – the South against the North at Lord's on 15 July 1850. Despite the fact that Wisden was born in Brighton, and was known as a Sussex cricketer, he still played for the North in this fixture, probably because of his connections with the All-England Eleven based in Nottingham. Twelve years later his sympathies with both North and South failed to head off the rebellion that eventually led him to give up playing cricket and begin writing about it. He was in his late thirties by this time, but still many years younger than Clarke had been at his wicket-taking peak, and might well have played for many more years if only his diplomatic skills had matched his entrepreneurial and cricketing ones.

The year 1864 is generally regarded as the starting point of modern cricket, not only because overarm bowling became legal but also because it was the year in which John Wisden published his first *Almanack*, the county championship got itself underway and W.G. Grace appeared in his first major match. W.G. Grace was the originator of modern batsmanship and modern bowling. The efforts of Clarke, Wisden and the

W. G. Grace – the originator of modern batsmanship and bowling.
Photograph by George Beldam

great county organisers had created a structure. All it needed
was a modern hero to popularise the game, and in W.G. it got
one. He was unquestionably the greatest British sportsman of
his century, and his influence stretches across all aspects of his
game and of organised sport in general. First of all, he was a

supreme athlete. People who have seen images only of a portly, bearded, greying gentleman looking uncomfortable with a cricket bat in hand will not realise that in his youth he was a great hurdler. At the end of July 1866, he was given time off from playing for England against Surrey at The Oval to take part in the National Olympian Sporting Association championships at the Crystal Palace. He won the 440 yards hurdles and then went back to the cricket match. He was not particularly needed, as England won by an innings and 296 runs, largely thanks to the 224 not out that the eighteen-year-old W.G. had scored before he had to rush off to become a hurdles champion. It had been his first first-class century.

The records that W.G. Grace established were not just those of a man who was a little bit better than most of his contemporaries. Grace was by such a distance the greatest player of his day that few men or women have ever matched his domination of his sport: he was the first man to score one hundred centuries, the first to score a triple century, the first man to score 1,000 runs before the end of May, the first man to score 2,000 runs in a season as many as six times, the first man to score 30,000, 40,000 and 50,000 first-class runs, the first man to take 2,000 first-class wickets, the first man to score a century and take ten wickets in the same match ten times, the first man to average over 50 with the bat in ten different seasons, the first man to achieve the double of 1,000 runs and 100 wickets in a season, a feat which he achieved eight times, the first man to score a century for England – the list goes on and on. In 1876, he made 839 runs in eight days, with consecutive scores of 344, 177 and 318 not out. He was incomparably the greatest cricketer of his lifetime.

Grace's influence on the tactics and techniques of cricket

was in many ways not as great as that of his elder brother, E. M. When "The Coroner" batted (for doctoring ran in the family, and it was a widely told joke that the family doctor, W.G., provided the coroner, E.M., with many of his most interesting cases), purists would look aghast, but the rest of the crowd would look at the scoreboard ticking up. If E.M. had not had a younger brother, he might well have been known as the greatest cricketer of his time. But while W.G. is thought of as a player who did everything correctly but better than his contemporaries, E.M. is remembered as a man who did everything differently from his contemporaries, and better than practically all of them except his brother. He was also exceptionally competitive; when playing against William Clarke's All-England Eleven at the age of only fourteen, he was given out leg before wicket. W.G.'s comment was simply, "I wonder if he was satisfied with the decision?" That was clearly what Latin teachers would call a *num* question, expecting the answer "no".

Dr Henry Grace had given his son E.M. a very large bat when he was still a young boy, and it was this outsize weapon which his Uncle Pocock blamed for his propensity for the pull shot. The traditional – or should we say classical – method of batting handed down by Nyren, Felix and their contemporaries clearly stated that balls delivered on the off side should be hit to the off and those delivered down the leg side should be hit to leg. E.M. just swung at balls outside his off stump and whacked them to the long-on boundary. This was fine at home in the Grace family orchard at Downend, because they had three dogs (Ponto, Noble and Don, the latter two coincidentally bearing the names of two of the greatest Australian cricketers of years to come) to fetch the balls back from the next-door field, the woods or the water. But at Lord's this was not considered the done thing. Still, he scored runs, just as seventy or eighty years later another country boy, Don Bradman, would come on to the world cricketing stage with a vicious and very profitable pull. Batsmen learned concentration from W.G. and improvisation from E.M.; bowlers had to learn how to cope with both.

E.M. and W.G. were not the end of the Grace family success. There was also the youngest brother, G. F., also known as Fred. In the first Test match ever played in England, there were three Grace brothers playing, the first and last time that three brothers have played for England together. Fred, in many ways as talented a cricketer as his elder brothers, was a tragic figure. In that first Test match, at The Oval on 6, 7 and 8 September 1880, W.G. made 152, putting on 91 for the first wicket with E.M., but Fred scored 0 in both innings, caught a cold at the end of the match and died within a fortnight. It was no consolation that he also caught one of the most famous catches of all time to dismiss the giant Australian Bonnor in the first innings of the game. The ball was hit so far and so high that the batsmen had completed two runs before it landed safely in G.F.'s hands.

Test match cricket in England started almost surreptitiously with that game in 1880. Englishmen had been playing cricket abroad for many years, and not only in places painted red on the map. In 1822, a game was played between the crews of HMS *Fury* and HMS *Hecla* "at Igloolik in the frozen North" according to one reliable source.[4] International cricket began in 1844, with Canada v the United States. The first international cricketer to die in battle was an American, Captain Walter Symonds Newhall of the 3rd Pennsylvanian Cavalry, who had played against Canada in 1859 and 1860, as well as against George Parr's visiting team from England in 1859. He died in the American Civil War in 1863, drowned in the Rappahannock

River in Virginia while fighting for the Union cause.

International sport had been part of the British sporting calendar for almost a decade by 1880, with annual football and rugby matches between the home nations. Representative cricket had been played already between an English touring team and an Australian eleven in 1877. In this match, which the Australians won by 45 runs, the English were without the services of their wicketkeeper, Ted Pooley, who had been detained in New Zealand earlier in the tour. Pooley, the best wicketkeeper but also one of the most argumentative men in England, never missed the chance of a drink or a bet. In New Zealand, he bet a local man, Ralph Donkin, one pound to a shilling that he could forecast the exact scores of every batsman in the next game the England touring team would play, against Eighteen of Canterbury. Donkin took the bet, and Pooley promptly forecast a duck for every player. After the match, Pooley claimed his pound for each duck and offered Donkin one shilling for each man (fewer than half the side, as it turned out) who got off the mark. By Pooley's reckoning, Donkin owed him about ten pounds. A fight ensued, Pooley was charged with assault and malicious damage, and he missed the boat to Australia and with it, his only chance of ever playing international cricket.

The man who organised the first Test match on English soil was Charles William Alcock JP, the first full-time, paid secretary of Surrey County Cricket Club. Alcock was the first professional sports administrator, and he was well in advance of his time in his ideas of what the public wanted. Born in 1842, he was a keen if not particularly talented cricketer, but a magnificent footballer, and a rugby player good enough to have played once for Blackheath. He was born in Sunderland but educated at Harrow, during the headmastership of Dr Vaughan, the man

Charles Alcock, a sporting all-rounder, was the first professional sports
administrator – a man well in advance of his time

who had decreed it "almost discreditable not to play, and play well at some game", with the result that Harrovians dominated the national stage in several sports in the middle years of the century. None were more dominant than Charles Alcock, who was a founder of the Wanderers Football Club, the founder and organiser of the Football Association Cup, captain of the Wanderers when they won the first FA Cup, referee of the 1875 final, captain of England's football team in its first internationals, and secretary of the Football Association from 1867. He was a vigorous and competitive sportsman, with a very physical presence on the football pitch. Alcock often described an incident when he was playing football with W.G. Grace (there was no end to W.G.'s sporting talents) for the Wanderers against Clapham Rovers.

"I had got the ball right in front of the Rovers goal and was just going to kick it between the posts when, in his great big rough sort of way, W.G. bowled me over and kicked the goal himself. It was the most blackguard thing that ever happened to me in the whole course of a sporting career." Grace replied by writing, "My behaviour on that occasion was not half as bad as Alcock's when playing at The Oval v Scotland [on 6 March 1875]. The way Alcock used to knock over a fellow when he was trying to pass him I shall never forget." He added that "Alcock made Catherine wheels of those fellows".

Muscular, moustachioed and energetic, Alcock organised football, rugby and even lacrosse at The Oval, as well as county cricket, making it the Wembley Stadium of its time. That first Test match had a very far-reaching effect. International sporting competition stretching beyond the British Isles had arrived, and was profitable. Every other sport noted the trend, and was impressed.

"I'M GOING TO PLAY SOCCER"

Charles Alcock transformed football with his invention of the Football Association Cup in 1872, but there were many pioneers of football in the earlier years of the century, without whom Alcock could never have operated. As late as 1880, a book on the sports of Britain included the message that "football has a hard fight. It meets its summer rival, cricket, on very disadvantageous terms. Climatic conditions alone tend greatly to impede its progress, while the want of unanimity amongst its followers goes far to prove that a house divided against itself cannot stand." But thanks to the spirit of organisation and order that swept across all Victorian sports and pastimes at this time, by the end of the century, football's claim to be the world's most popular sport was beginning to be asserted. Another century later, there can be no doubt of its pre-eminence.

At the beginning of the 19th century, football had all but died out as a public sport. It was disorganised and vicious and it distracted otherwise hardworking people from what they ought to be doing, i.e. working for their mill-owner or their agricultural landlord. Joseph Strutt (1749–1802), noted in his *Sports and Pastimes of the People of England* that "when the exercise becomes exceedingly violent, the players kick each other's shins". Its survival and revival was almost entirely due to the public-school system. Thus it was that football developed during the 19th century from an excuse for public street rioting into a manly game for sons of gentlefolk. But it was at first a shambolic growth.

The point about football is that it is easy to get a game going. The skills are basic – kicking, running and barging into other players. The equipment is simple – a ball and somewhere vaguely flat to play. The rules are very easy to understand, especially when there are no rules except that the ball has to find its way into the goal for one team to win. In the early 1800s, it was also the perfect way for high-spirited young men to run off their excess energy, and for the bigger boys to dominate the smaller ones, as was traditional in the public-school system at the time. So the game, in different forms at different schools, had become the most popular winter sport by the time Queen Victoria came to the throne.

Each school played the game a little bit differently from every other school, but this was not seen at first as a particular problem. After all, the game was only going to be played at school, and inter-school fixtures were a rarity. So provided everybody at each school knew the local conventions, there was no confusion. What did it matter if Eton played the game alongside a high wall, that Westminster used a couple of trees as the goalposts or that Charterhouse played the game within the cloisters, using the walls and buttresses as features of the play? If at the King's School Canterbury, players had to become adept at sidestepping the trees and railings, while at Harrow they tried to kick the ball right over the buildings, what difference did it make? The only thing all these games had in common was their name. They were all called football because in every game, there was a ball and there were feet.

The features which made each school's version of football original also tended to increase school unity and spirit among the pupils, who could compare their game with those played elsewhere and extol the virtues of their own version. Anything which gave the pupils some sense of pride in their own school was not completely frowned upon by the schoolmasters, which is perhaps why football survived. With its almost total lack of rules, it also required little supervision, another virtue in the eyes of the hard-pressed teaching staff. Almost without realising it, the schools were creating a game and an ethos which would sweep the world. By the end of the millennium this game would be inspiring something more than a simple sense of pride and team spirit. It would become a matter for blind chauvinism and fanatical local support.

When the old boys of these schools arrived at their universities, they discovered that games of football were impossible to organise. So it was there that the first moves were made to create a national game of football which everybody could play. For many years the problem had been ignored at Oxford and Cambridge because most undergraduates took their exercise by riding or rowing rather than kicking a ball, but this could not last for long once the new enthusiasm for football caught hold at the public schools. The university men were not trying to invent a new game to supersede the schools' versions of football. At no stage did they imagine that by creating a standard version of the game, they would kill off other versions; they just wanted to be able to play with people who had been brought up in different parts of the country without having to argue about the rules.

In the 1840s, the first serious attempt at creating a set of rules for football which would allow the game to be played anywhere was made by a group of Cambridge undergraduates, one of whom went on to earn for himself a central position in the history of the development of the game. This was Charles Thring, an old boy of Shrewsbury School. Thring had been at Shrewsbury under the headmastership of Dr Samuel Butler, a man who so disapproved of all sporting activities that he went out of his way to stop football at his school. His efforts had obviously been useless in the case of Thring. Dr Butler described Shrewsbury's football as "more fit for farm boys and labourers than young gentlemen", but the young gentlemen went on playing it all the same.

In 1839, an undergraduate named Albert Pell had formed, or tried to form, the first football club at Cambridge University. He met with opposition and derision, and more importantly a great deal of confusion about what game they were supposed to be playing. Pell was an Old Rugbeian who therefore favoured the handling game, but as the football club came to be dominated by Etonians who preferred to kick the ball, it was inevitable that confusion reigned. In 1846, Charles Thring and a Shrewsbury colleague named de Winton tried to carry on the work that Arthur Pell had started, but their version of the game was dismissed by the Etonians as not worth playing, and the game became mired in local rivalries and disagreements.

The story of how the "Cambridge Rules" of 1848 were developed has been told by Henry C. Malden, a Trinity College second-year undergraduate who chaired the meetings between the undergraduate old boys of at least five public schools. Malden had himself been privately educated, so was considered an impartial chairman. In a letter dated 1897, half a century after the events he describes, Malden says that "an attempt was made to get up some football in preference to the hockey then in vogue", though it remains a mystery why hockey should have been more popular, when it too had not been properly codified at that time.

The men who were giving themselves the responsibility of putting together some unified rules for football were all in their teens or early twenties, and had no motivation other than to be able to play football together in harmony. Still, they took themselves and their task very seriously, in the spirit of the times. It was decided that two men would represent each of the public schools, and Malden remembers that there were a total of fourteen in all. Two of the delegates were Malden and a man named Salt, who had also been privately educated, and these two were meant to keep the different public-school factions from each other's throats. He recalled how "the Eton men howled at the Rugby men for handling the ball". The public schools represented were, in Malden's account, Harrow, Eton, Rugby, Winchester and Shrewsbury. If there were two delegates from each school, this brings the total to twelve, not fourteen, so we can assume another school, probably Charterhouse or Westminster, was also represented; or else that Malden was not reading mathematics.

The meeting, in Malden's rooms, lasted from four o'clock in the afternoon until just before midnight, which Malden thought was a very long time to agree a set of rules, but which these days would have been thought barely long enough to decide upon the seating arrangements or the shape of the table, let alone the order of items on the agenda. The new rules were printed up as Cambridge Rules and published around the university, and "very satisfactorily they worked, for it is right to add that they were loyally kept and I never heard of any Public School man who gave up playing from not liking the rules." Malden's account is not an impartial one, but all the same, the

Cambridge Rules mark the beginnings of football as we know it today. Their influence outside Cambridge was probably slight at best, and most accounts seem to agree that they faded into obscurity once their originators had graduated; but this was the first attempt anywhere to codify a game that was never likely to be universally popular until and unless there was a set of universal rules.

The Cambridge Rules were based much more on the Harrow style of play than the Rugby style. Catching and running with the ball was not allowed and hacking was discouraged. Charles Thring, one of the fourteen cooped up in Henry Malden's room that evening in 1848, took holy orders on graduation and became a teacher. By 1862 he was on the staff of Uppingham School in Rutland, where his brother Edward was the headmaster. Edward Thring, an Old Etonian and like his younger brother an ordained priest, had been headmaster at Uppingham since 1853, and appointed his brother to the staff in 1859. The Reverend Edward had tried to codify the rules for football at the school before the Reverend Charles arrived, but Charles was an evangelical enthusiast for a universal code for football, and with great fervour, he took on the task of issuing a set of rules which he wanted the school to use.

In 1862, he published a set of rules that he alone had authored, but which were fairly closely based on the Cambridge Rules that he had helped to devise fourteen years before. He called his code, 'The Simplest Game', partly because there were only ten rules.

Rule 1 covered scoring: "A goal is scored whenever the ball is forced through the goal and under the bar, except it be thrown by the hand." So Diego Maradona's tactics were outlawed from the very start. Rule 2 explained that "hands may be used only to stop a ball and place it on the ground before the feet", but at this stage, at least, anybody was allowed to handle the ball, not just the goalkeeper. Rule 3 outlawed hacking: "Kicks must be aimed only at the ball." Rule 4 is more obscure to modern eyes, explaining that "a player may not kick the ball whilst in the air". Is this while the ball is in the air or while the player is in the air? And what of the bouncing ball?

Rule 5 takes us back to physical violence: "No tripping or heel-kicking allowed", a rule which is still in theory in place today, although to watch professional football from the terraces or on the television, you could be forgiven for thinking otherwise. Rules 6 to 9 covered more abstruse moments in play, notably the early equivalent of a throw-in, "whenever a ball is kicked beyond the side flags, it must be returned by the player who kicked it from the spot it passed the flag line in a straight line towards the middle of the ground"; the goalkick, "when a ball is kicked behind the line of goal, it shall be kicked off from that line by one of the side whose goal it is; "no player may stand within six paces of the kicker when he is kicking-off"; and the early rumblings of an offside law, "a player is out of play immediately he is in front of the ball, and must return behind the ball as soon as possible. If the ball is kicked by his own side past a player, he may not touch it, or advance, until one of the other side has first kicked it, or one of his own side, having followed it up, has been able, when in front of him, to kick it." This sounds remarkably like the rugby offside law, rather than the football one, and it explains why even with these rules, the split between the two styles of play was not yet complete.

Rule 10, the last on Thring's little list, turned again to the question of brute force: "No charging is allowed when a player is out of play, i.e. immediately the ball is behind him." There is no problem about charging the man whether or not he has the ball, just as long as he is in play. This was certainly Christianity at its most muscular. But the new rules contained nothing about the size or markings of the pitch, the number of players on each side nor the length of the game. There was nothing about substitutes, a feature that was not important when teams were of up to two hundred a side as at Rugby School, for example, but which would have significance in a very physical eleven-a-side game. There was no mention of the referee, of half-times and changing ends, of corner kicks, the shape and size of the ball or many other obvious elements of football today. But it was a start.

In November 1862, a match took place at Cambridge between Cambridge Old Etonians and Cambridge Old Harrovians, playing to Charles Thring's rules. The game was eleven a side, with an umpire from each side as well as an impartial referee. The goals were twelve feet wide and the game lasted for seventy-five minutes, with a change of ends every time a goal was scored. The rules of a game quite similar to the game we know today were put to the test, and they worked. The basis of the first laws adopted by the Football Association a year later was in place.

It was fortunate for Charles Thring that he was a priest, because that meant he would have known the Gospel according to St Matthew, notably chapter 13, verse 57, which says that "a prophet is not without honour, save in his own country". His simplest rules set in motion a chain of events that just one year later led to the formation of the Football Association, but at Uppingham his brother the Reverend Edward was much less enthusiastic. In 1863, Charles applied on behalf of Uppingham to join the newly formed Association. The application from such a well-known and active proponent of the new code would certainly have been accepted, had not the Reverend Edward decided that games against other clubs and schools would be giving them a prominence in his school's curriculum that he did not wish them to have. He therefore instructed the Reverend Charles to withdraw the application to join. Charles left Uppingham in a sulk in 1864, and the school carried on playing its own version of the game, which was neither Etonian nor Salopian, neither soccer nor rugger in style, but involved fifteen players a side, an oval-shaped ball and a goal forty feet wide and seven feet high.

On Monday 26 October 1863, a meeting took place at the Freemasons Tavern in Great Queen Street, Lincolns Inn Fields, London, barely a short back-heel from where the third Duke of Bolton had first set eyes on Lavinia Fenton a hundred and thirty-five years earlier. The meeting was called by Ebenezer Cobb Morley, who had founded the Barnes Football Club a year earlier, in order to form an association of football clubs "with the object of establishing a definite code of rules for the regulation of the game". Twelve clubs were represented at that first meeting: Barnes, Blackheath, Blackheath School, Charterhouse School, Crystal Palace, Crusaders, Forest, Kensington School, No Names of Kilburn, Perceval House of Blackheath, Surbiton and the War Office Club – no Uppingham, no universities and no representatives of any of the urban clubs that were forming north of a line from Bristol to the Wash. The Charterhouse representative was B.F. Hartshorne, the eighteen-year-old captain of the school eleven. One of the two Forest representatives was J.F. Alcock, whose brother Charles was to become the guiding light of the infant association. The Victorian ideal of the family as the basis of society was certainly reflected in the organisation of sport.

The meeting quickly voted to create the Football Association. Ebenezer Morley was elected secretary, Arthur Pember of the No Names was elected president, and eleven of the twelve clubs paid their first subscription of a guinea there and then. The odd one out was Charterhouse, according to some historians because they were "biding their time", but just as likely because the schoolboy Hartshorne just did not have a guinea on him. Over the next six weeks there were six meetings held to codify the game, based strongly around Thring's ten simple rules, and it was after the sixth of these, on 8 December 1863, that Blackheath resigned from the Association because they wanted hacking to be part of the game and the others did not.

It is very unlikely that anybody thought that the infant Association would have anything other than a regional influence as an enabling institution which would organise fixtures between clubs and allow young men to enjoy healthy exercise. Other sporting organisations thought it was unimportant, one Oxford man denigrating the Association and the sport by noting in a letter to the *Sporting Life* that the participants of the meetings which were still going on were "not of sufficient consequence to cause their suggestions to be generally acted upon". It looks very much as though this particular correspondent was protesting too much, for he at least was taking note of what was going on, and thought it of sufficient consequence to fire a broadside in the columns of a newspaper. Perhaps it was just the natural reaction of an Oxford man to the goings-on in a sport where Cambridge had traditionally taken the lead.

The purpose of the FA was not to impose their laws on all clubs, or to attempt to control the games that were played around the country. They had established a friendly playing relationship with the Sheffield Football Club, founded in 1855, which soon became the only member of the Association farther afield than the home counties. The infant FA began to push out the boundaries of its influence from 1866, when Charles Alcock succeeded his brother as Forest's representative at the Football Association. By this time, the FA rules were catching on around the country, especially among the officers in the more fashion-able regiments of armed forces, and increasingly among the working men's clubs of the Midlands and the industrial North. The leaders in this were from the same background as most of the members of the Football Association in London; they were public schoolboys and Oxbridge graduates who had gone into the church and were now in charge of what we would call these days inner-city parishes.

Half-day working on Saturday became the norm in facto-ries from the mid-1850s, and this gave the workers time to indulge in short but strenuous exercise. The obvious candidate to fill this need was football, which was now available in two varieties. The Association version won out in most parts of the country because, firstly, it was indeed the simplest game and, secondly, it was less violent. Although the Blackheath represen-tative at the early association meetings had waxed lyrical about the fact that "in former years men were so wounded that two of them were actually carried off the field", the more common attitude to rugby was expressed by the Sheffield Football Club, which compared it more to Cornish wrestling than football. The average working man preferred the kicking game to the handling one. There was a limit to the working man's idea of muscular Christianity.

It is easy to forget, or not to consider, the role the church played in Victorian society. The Sunday sermon was a major spectator event, listened to and discussed as much as any episode of *Coronation Street* would be today. The sermons of great preachers like Cardinal Newman or Charles Spurgeon were published and read by millions, and talked about by all classes of society. The church, whether represented by the established Church of England, the still not-quite-respectable Roman Catholics or the wide variety of non-conformist churches was still the main source of local information and of community spirit for all people. As Marshall McLuhan would have noted, the church was the medium and the church was the message.

So it is perhaps not surprising that so many of the leading clubs of today began as offshoots of churches or board schools, inspired by the enthusiasm of their local priests. Reverend Gordon Young was the founder of Queens Park Rangers, which began life as an outlet for the footballing skills of the boys of the Droop Street Board School. It became Queens Park Rangers when two other religious institution clubs, Christchurch Rangers and St Jude's Institute FC, joined forces with the Reverend Young's men. The Reverend Tiverton Preedy, curate of St Peter's in Barnsley, was the leading light in the formation of what is now Barnsley FC. The Christ Church Sunday School in Blackburn Street, Bolton, formed Christ Church FC whose president was the vicar. When the vicar found it difficult to reconcile the use of church land for football, the players broke away from the church and created Bolton Wanderers, the name deriving from their lack of a pitch. Swindon Town was founded by the Reverend William Pitt, as the Spartans who subsequently merged with St Mark's Young Men's Friendly Society.

Bournemouth began as Boscombe St John's; Wolverhampton Wanderers began as a club for members of St Luke's Church, Blakenhall; Southampton are still known as the Saints from their early connection with St Mary's Church; and many other clubs have Methodist or other non-conformist origins. Villa Cross Wesleyan Chapel in Aston was the starting point for Aston Villa; Bury Unitarians and Bury Wesleyans combined to form the rather less adventurously named Bury FC; Stockport County was formed by members of Wycliffe Congregational Chapel; and Tottenham Hotspur's first home was the local YMCA. Of the ninety-two clubs in the Premier League and the Football League in 1998, perhaps eighteen can trace their origins clearly to the church, and another dozen or so were formed by old boys of schools with strong religious connections. For a sport that these days is seen by some as a symbol of the degeneration of public morals, it is a remarkable heritage.

Reading Football Club is the oldest league club south of the Trent, and yet it was not formed until 1871, the same year that Charles Alcock came up with the idea that had a greater impact on the social history of the 20th century than almost any other. A case could be made for the invention of the motor car, the birth of Adolf Hitler or the ideas of Einstein which led inexorably to the invention of the atom bomb, but if we are looking for a simple device that changed the leisure hours of almost everybody on the planet, then Alcock's proposal on 20 July 1871 to his fellow committee members must be on anybody's short list.

His proposal was made at a meeting in the offices of *The Sportsman* newspaper, just off Fleet Street, and his fellow committee members present that evening were the Football Association treasurer Mr A. Stair, Mr D. Allport representing Crystal Palace FC, Mr M.P. Betts of the Harrow Chequers, Mr J.H. Giffard of the Civil Service Club, Captain Francis Marindin of the Royal Engineers and Mr C.W. Stephenson of

Westminster School. Marindin and Betts would go on to play central roles in the development of the Football Association, but it was Charles Alcock, who was also at this time a regular journalist at *The Sportsman* as well as secretary of Surrey County Cricket Club, whose idea changed the footballing world.

His motion put forward to the committee was "that it is desirable that a Challenge Cup should be established in connection with the Association, for which all clubs belonging to the Association should be invited to compete". The idea of a sudden-death, knock-out competition would have been nothing new to Alcock, who had experienced the Cock House competitions at Harrow, which worked on the same principle. He no doubt had to explain the way he saw it working, but he must have done it well. The motion was carried very quickly. By October, a cup had been ordered at the substantial cost of twenty pounds from Martin, Hall and Co., and the rules of the competition had been drafted, agreed and circulated to the fifty or so clubs that were by then members of the Association. Of those fifty, only fifteen decided to enter, but the geographical spread was as broad as could be expected, and indeed almost greater than it is these days. Thirteen of the clubs were from London and the home counties – confirming the amateur and gentrified image of the Football Association in direct contrast to the working-class teams in the Midlands and the North. Two of the clubs were from further north, but both were spiritually close to the ethos of the Football Association, even if geographically they were farther afield. They were Donington Grammar School from Spalding in Lincolnshire and Queen's Park, the great amateur side from Glasgow.

Queen's Park are the only one of the teams entering for that first FA Cup still playing senior football today. Even Donington

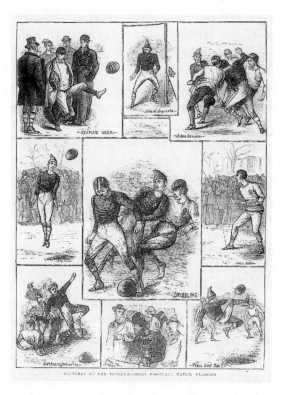

England v Scotland, at the West of Scotland cricket club,
near Glasgow, 1872. These encounters played a key role in the early
development of Association football

Grammar School has become Donington Secondary School,
and the Crystal Palace that entered in 1871 is not the Crystal
Palace club that reached the Cup final in 1990. It may seem odd
today to think of a Glasgow team playing in the English FA
Cup, but in 1871, there was no Scottish FA, and the Glasgow
side, as amateurs and members of the only Football Association

in Britain, were entitled to enter. What is more, they should have been favourites to win. The club, formed in 1867, was the first football club in Scotland, which explains why they did not play their first competitive game until a year later. They had to wait until other clubs were formed for them to play against. Once they started playing against other sides, they swept all before them. They did not lose a game, or even concede a goal for the first five years of their existence, a remarkable run that was still in full flow in the autumn of 1871.

Because there were only fifteen teams, a straight knock-out could not be arranged, but the obvious idea of fourteen teams playing a first round and one side getting a bye to give eight sides in the next round was not considered. Maybe they did not do things that way in the Harrow Cock House competition. So on 11 November 1871, the first ties were played: Upton Park against Clapham Rovers, Barnes versus the Civil Service, Maidenhead against Marlow and Crystal Palace versus Hitchin. Clapham Rovers beat Upton Park 3–0, with Jarvis Kenrick of Clapham gaining some kind of immortality by scoring the first goal ever scored in the competition. Barnes were 2–0 winners against the Civil Service, and Maidenhead beat Marlow by the same score. Crystal Palace and Hitchin played out a goalless draw, so both teams advanced to the next round. To simplify the travel problems, Queen's Park and Donington Grammar School were drawn against each other, but still could not find a suitable date on which to play. So they were both given a bye to the next round and told to play again. At this point, Donington gave Queen's Park a walkover. That was the end of Donington Grammar School's entire FA Cup experience, for they never entered again.

The Wanderers, Charles Alcock's club, were due to play the

Harrow Chequers on that first Cup Saturday, 11 November, but Harrow Chequers could not raise a side, and Wanderers advanced with a walkover. The Harrow Chequers were obviously very much of the Donington Grammar tradition of doughty Cup fighters, because after their first disaster, they entered twice more, in 1874 and 1875, but scratched both times. They remain the only side to have entered the FA Cup three times and never to have suffered a defeat. One Harrow Chequer, Morton Peto Betts, who had been one of the committee who had listened to Alcock's first proposal, still had a part to play in the 1871–1872 competition, though.

Reigate Priory, like Donington and Harrow, scratched to give the Royal Engineers a free ride into the next round, and the Hampstead Heathens were given a bye. The first round had reduced the original fifteen to a mere ten. In the next round, Donington Grammar, Hitchin, Clapham Rovers, Barnes and Maidenhead were all eliminated, and the Royal Engineers, led by the imposing Captain Marindin, looked by far the strongest side on show. The next round, with just five teams remaining, reduced this number to four by the simple process of giving Queen's Park a bye because nobody wanted to go up to Scotland to play them, and by allowing both Crystal Palace and the Wanderers, who managed a 0–0 draw, to go through to the semi-final. Only the Hampstead Heathens were eliminated, beaten 3–0 by the impressive Royal Engineers.

The semi-finals were dull. The Royal Engineers beat Crystal Palace 3–0 in a replay after a 0–0 draw, and the Wanderers sailed through when Queen's Park dropped out of the competition after a 0–0 draw at The Oval. It was said at the time that Queen's Park had had to pass the hat round to raise the four pounds required to get to London for the semi-final tie, and although they could obviously have afforded to play the Wanderers at home, they could not have afforded to come back to London for the final, and therefore dropped out. The luck of the Wanderers, ably led by Charles Alcock, was continuing.

So the final, on 16 March 1872, was between the Royal Engineers, the hot favourites, and the Wanderers. The match was played at the Wanderers' home ground, Kennington Oval, in front of a crowd of around two thousand people, which seems to be the favourite estimate for all decent-sized sporting crowds in the latter part of the 19th century. As was to happen many times in future finals, the favourites were beaten, and an injury was a deciding factor. Within ten minutes, Lt Edmund Cresswell had fallen down and broken his collar bone. We do not know whether this was after a collision with the forceful Alcock, but it meant that for the rest of the game Cresswell was a passenger on the wing. Five minutes later, the soon-to-be Reverend Robert Vidal, an old boy of Westminster School rejoicing in the hard-earned title of "the prince of the dribblers", got the ball and passed it to Morton Betts, who thumped it past Captain William Merriman, the RE goalkeeper. Betts, having been listed in the Harrow Chequers team that scratched against the Wanderers in the first round, was shy about boasting of his success for another club. The goal was therefore recorded for posterity as having been scored by "A H Chequer", standing for "A Harrow Chequer". Had the first-round tie actually been played, and assuming that the Wanderers had still won, under present competition rules, Betts would have been cup-tied and unable to play for another team in the same season's competition. However, in 1871, such rules had not been considered.

Betts's goal was the only one of the match, 1–0 to the Wanderers, although it might have been 2–0 if Charles Alcock's goal a little later had not been disallowed. There was, so the reports tell us, more than a suggestion of handball in his goal, but in the end it did not matter. Charles Alcock was able to lift his own Cup on his own home ground. He was satisfied that his new idea was a success. He had a Cup-winner's medal, his employer Surrey County Cricket Club had another lucrative fixture on their home ground, and the amateurs of British football had proved themselves at least better organisers than the northerners who were playing a brand of football that looked suspiciously as though it might be professional.

Alcock was not alone in his missionary zeal to spread the influence of the Football Association around the country. There were in particular two other remarkable men who played and organised the game with at least as much energy as Alcock. Captain Marindin, on the losing side in the first final, rose to the rank of major, but his lasting claim to fame is not a military one. Marindin played for both the Royal Engineers and the Old Etonians, whose football club he founded, so when the two teams met in the final of 1875, by which time Marindin was also president of the FA, he decided to play for neither of them. That was the only year during Marindin's playing days that either of his teams won the Cup, so he did himself out of a winner's medal. But he featured in many more finals as referee, nine times in the 1880s. He ended up as Sir Francis Marindin, knighted for his services as Inspector of Railways as much as for his football.

The Hon. Arthur Fitzgerald Kinnaird was an Old Etonian and friend of Alcock's, and he played in nine finals (plus two replayed finals), three for the Wanderers and six for the Old Etonians. He was an unmistakable figure with his full beard, and he dominated the midfield. He was a winner five times, but

Culture clash – the gentlemen of Old Etonians beaten by Blackburn Olympic
from the industrial north in the Football Association Challenge Cup 1883

only once in a match refereed by Major Marindin. If he ever
played in the same game as that other Victorian sporting hero,
W.G. Grace (which is entirely possible, because we know that
Grace played on the same football team as Charles Alcock from
time to time), the sight of these two selfish and physical bearded giants chasing after the same ball would have been something
to treasure. In 1887, five years after his fifth winning final,
Arthur succeeded his father to the family title, and became the
eleventh Baron Kinnaird. He never became a priest, but his
interest in muscular Christianity is clear from his presidency of
the Young Men's Christian Association and other evangelical
movements, of which he no doubt counted the Football
Association as one.

While these fine English gentlemen were running the Football Association in London, a separate movement was gathering force in Scotland and the industrial North. Alcock, Marindin and Kinnaird (who was in any case Scottish and captain of Scotland in their second football international) viewed it with interest but no real opposition, although there were some people who felt that football, like cricket, rugby, racing and the rest, should be kept in the hands of the ruling classes who would know how to develop it properly. The argument from the southern viewpoint was succinctly put, but rather too late, by *Badminton* magazine in 1896: "The artisan differs from the public-school man in two important points: he plays to win at all costs, and from the nature of his associations he steps on to the football field in better training." Win at all costs! What a contemptible idea! They might even decide it is worth paying people to help them win.

For the northern and Midlands "artisans", football was not an exercise to show off the moral superiority of the upper classes, nor was it an extension of religious worship. It was a development of the mediaeval games of village football, which still retained a place in the collective memory and in some parts of Britain were still played from time to time. These games were frowned on by the authorities, so they had the added attraction of being dangerous both physically and socially, and this sense of cocking a snook at the powers that be was certainly one reason why football had always claimed a foothold among the less obeisant Britons who lived north of Watford. There was a passion about football that did not exist in the more sedate games of cricket and golf, and never was allowed to develop in the new Victorian games of tennis and rugby. It was shirts that were tugged on the football pitch, not forelocks.

It was also a glorious release from the rigours of the working week, for both players and, more importantly for the financial solvency of the game, for spectators too. By the time the FA Cup competition was beginning to work well, and northern clubs like Blackburn Rovers were winning it, there were the first stirrings of professionalism and a growing desire to watch top-class football on a regular basis. It was into this situation that William McGregor, a Scotsman then based in Birmingham, stepped boldly in 1888. Since 1882, when the Old Etonians won the FA Cup for the last time, the prize had gone north every year, and was to continue to do so until Tottenham Hotspur won the Cup back for London in 1901, so there was every justification for the belief that football in the North was stronger than in the home counties.

Spurs were at that time not a member of the organisation for which McGregor is rightly remembered, the Football League, but 1901 was the last time that any club from outside McGregor's League was to win the FA Cup until it split into two different organisations in the 1990s. The idea of a League was not original to McGregor, as there were already similar tournaments in American baseball, and county cricket had recently organised itself along league tournament lines. However, before the Football League was formed, matches were played in what the official history of the League calls "a more or less casual, haphazard way".[1] This did nothing to promote public interest in the game, for very often spectators would turn up at a ground ready to watch a game, only to learn that the visitors had missed their train connection, or could not raise a team; at any rate, there would be no game that day. The Football League was meant to put an end to all that, and in the end it did.

William McGregor, founder of the Football League

In the 1870s, Scottish players began to appear for Lancashire clubs, and there seemed to be little doubt that these men, skilled in the arts of the passing game which had made Queen's Park such a force north of the border, were being paid to play. The usual excuse made by the clubs they played for was that they had "missed their train home", but most people knew they hadn't even stood on the platform waiting. This was anathema to the Football Association, but the more pragmatic businessmen who owned the northern clubs saw nothing wrong in it. The organisers of the League chided the Football Association for its "parochial, or at all events a Metropolitan, appeal", but their League was no more widespread at the beginning. Sheffield, which was the only northern city in which the Football Association had a really loyal following, stayed away from the new League, leaving both Wednesday and United forced to apply for membership four years later in 1892 when the infant League was so successful that it needed a larger playpen.

This was one of the few occasions when the Sheffield footballers were seen to back the wrong horse, as they had a reputation for being at the forefront of developing the sport throughout the period. The first floodlit game, for example, took place at Sheffield United's ground, Bramall Lane, on 14 October 1878, when two teams played a demonstration game in front of a crowd estimated as "nearly twenty thousand" on a chilly moonlit night. The floodlights were on thirty-foot high wooden towers, and the experiment was deemed a success. Further trial games under floodlights took place over the next few weeks at other grounds, but it was many years before floodlit league or Cup games were allowed. In 1930, over half a century after this experiment, the FA actually banned floodlit Cup games, and it was not until 1955 that the first floodlit games were played in the Cup, three-quarters of a century after they had been first tried out.

Half the original members of the League were from a small area of Lancashire (Preston, Bolton, Burnley, Accrington, Blackburn and Everton) and the others were from the Midlands (Stoke, Derby, Wolverhampton, West Bromwich, Aston Villa and Notts County). Only two clubs from farther south, Arsenal and Luton Town, joined the League before the turn of the century. There was a clear divide between the northern, professional, League and the southern, amateur, Association. However, because they had agreed on a set of laws for the "simplest game", and because the Football League had written into their first set of rules "that all matches should be played under the Cup rules of the Football Association", no final split occurred.

The League was as haphazard as the FA Cup competition when it first began. It was not until after the 1888–1889 season began that they even decided on the points system, which would decide the champion team at the end of the season. On 21 November 1888, by which time most sides had already played as many as ten of their twenty-two matches, it was decided, by a slim majority of six votes to four, that there would be "two points for a win and one for a draw. In the event of two or more clubs equal in points, the best goal average to count." The alternative, put forward by Louis Ford of West Bromwich Albion, was that everything except a win should be ignored.

At Preston North End, where on 15 October 1887 they had recorded the largest victory in English senior football when they beat Hyde United 26–0 in the first round of the Cup, there was the first concerted attempt to create the perfect football team. It worked, because Preston won both the League in its first season – without losing a game – and the Cup without conceding a goal. So the die was cast, and many teams have since then tried to follow their example and create all-powerful teams, using the weapon that was first used in earnest by the driving force behind Preston North End who was also the first treasurer of the Football League, Major William Sudell. That weapon was money.

William Sudell was a bit of a villain. He was a member of the original Football League management committee, despite his position in the years before the League was formed as "the head and front of the illegal movement of the early eighties which brought about professionalism", to quote the words of the official history of the League. Sudell, like most doubtful characters of the times, used his army rank in civilian life, although it is unclear how he managed to be promoted from captain, as he styled himself in the early 1880s, to major, which he had become by 1888. His aim was to create an invincible team, and his motivation for doing so seems to have been an obsession with beating Blackburn Rovers.

Preston North End grew out of the North End Cricket and Rugby Club which was formed in 1863. They played a little of everything before getting round to soccer around 1879. (As an aside, the game would not have been known as "soccer" at this time, the abbreviation being coined by an Oxford undergraduate, Charles Wreford Brown, in the late 1880s. Brown played football for England as an undergraduate in 1889, and some time before that, when asked if he wanted a game of "rugger", replied, "No thanks, I'm going to play soccer." But since that time, all real aficionados of the game continue to call it football rather than soccer, just as rugby players call their game rugby rather than rugger. Both codes are considered by their followers to be the "true" version of the ancient game of football.) Early in 1881, Preston North End decided to switch to football to the exclusion of all other sports, and on 26 March that year they must have wondered whether they made the right decision when they were beaten 16–0 by the strongest team in Lancashire, Blackburn Rovers. Preston North End's determination to be the best seems to have stemmed from this thrashing.

Sudell was certainly not the first man to resort to paying players, or to buying them from other clubs; this had been going on for a few seasons as clubs strove for supremacy. But he was the first to admit it openly and the first to go about building a team systematically. He brought Nicholas Ross to Preston from Heart of Midlothian in Scotland in 1883, and from then on took his shopping list around the country to make sure Preston would win at all costs, that most undignified professional aim which really was not what the Victorian gentleman sportsman ought to be thinking about. In 1883 and 1884, Accrington were disqualified from the FA Cup for professionalism, a fate which awaited Preston North End in 1884. These disqualifications turned out to be the dying throes of the amateur ethos, because the years 1884 and 1885 marked the turning point towards the ultimate victory of professionalism. In January 1884, Preston drew 1–1 with Upton Park in the fourth round of the competition, only for Upton Park to complain that they were fielding professionals. Sudell did not deny the charge; he simply asked how else could Preston keep up with Blackburn Rovers? The local press took up his cause, and the FA committee realised that professionalism was a force that could not be stopped. Still, they disqualified Preston North End, who decided that if their professionals were not wanted by the FA, they would not enter the competition the following year.

On 20 July 1885, professionalism was recognised by the Football Association, although the first professional to play for England, James Forrest of Blackburn Rovers, had jumped the gun by playing against Wales on 17 March 1884. It was not until his fourth international appearance, against Scotland on 21 March 1885, that his professional status was called into question, the Scots believing it unfair for England to field professionals. This shows the influence of the avowedly amateur Queen's Park club, because their protest made no sense. After all, most of the professionals in the English football league were Scots. Perhaps it was because Scotland only managed a 1–1 draw, the first time Scotland had not won the annual encounter since 1879 – but of course, the amateur ethic is not to win at all costs; that's the professional viewpoint. When the two teams met again, in Glasgow on 31 March 1886, Scottish sensitivities

A drawing from 1879 of an England v. Scotland match at Kennington Oval shows the sagging tape that was used between the posts before the introduction of the crossbar

were pandered to. Forrest was made to wear a much tighter shirt than his amateur team-mates, so that he could be easily distinguished as a professional. This bizarre distinction did not seem to slow down his play. Forrest was a very skinny and fit person, so the shirt must have been ludicrously small to look tight over his wiry frame. Why didn't they just go the whole hog and paint a pound sign on his forehead? The concept of branding professionals was dropped almost immediately. Soon they outnumbered the amateurs in the national sides, but there was, not surprisingly, no attempt to turn the spotlight on the amateurs by their dress code.

William Sudell's dream of creating the Invincibles came true in 1888–1889, when not only was he the treasurer of the Football League, but his team won both the league title and the FA Cup. There were few Englishmen in his side; he relied on a Scottish half-back line, a Welsh goalkeeper and only five Englishmen, a remarkably low count for the time. Sudell was undoubtedly a huge influence on the development of the professional game in Britain, but he was also a fraud. His time as Hon. Treasurer of the Football League came to a sudden end after only three years when the offices of secretary and treasurer were amalgamated, and the incumbent secretary, Harry Lockett of Stoke, took over the post. The official history of the Football League glides easily over this change in hierarchy, but the astute reader will notice that the only man who served on that original committee who does not rate a photograph in the self-congratulatory chapter on "The Management and its Personnel" is William Sudell. This may be because by this time he had served time in prison for fraud. There are photographs of him which still exist, showing a tall rather smooth, clean-shaven man, looking far younger and more energetic than his fellow administrators; a shrewd, unscrupulous charmer determined to achieve his goals by whatever means it took.

By the end of the century, many rule changes and several inventions of items of playing equipment had occurred, bringing football even closer to the game we watch and play today. The shape and size of the football (a circumference of 69–71 cms at the start of the game, and a weight of 396–453 grams) was settled only in 1872, the year of the first FA Cup competition, and the referee's whistle was not used until 1878. Shin pads were invented by Sam Widdowson of Nottingham Forest in 1874. The club was at the time officially called Nottingham Forest Football and Bandy Club, bandy being a sort of hockey played on an ice-covered football pitch. Playing bandy was definitely hard on the shins, so Mr Widdowson's invention was greeted with cries of acclamation by his clubmates, and quickly spread throughout football. Crossbars replaced flimsy and sagging tapes across the top of the goalposts in 1875, but goal nets – the invention of a Mr Brodie of Liverpool – did not come into common use until much later, being first officially used in a match between the North and the South in 1891. The 36–0 victory by Arbroath over Bon Accord in the Scottish FA Cup competition of 1885–1886 would probably have been even more convincing if the ball had been collected in the back of a net, rather than being blasted between the posts and into the crowd every time Arbroath scored. The *Dundee Courier and Argus* reported that the Arbroath goalkeeper, Milne, "neither touched the ball with hand or foot during the match, but remained under the friendly shelter of an umbrella the whole time".

Rule changes as well as equipment changes came thick and fast during the first years of League and Cup football. In 1882,

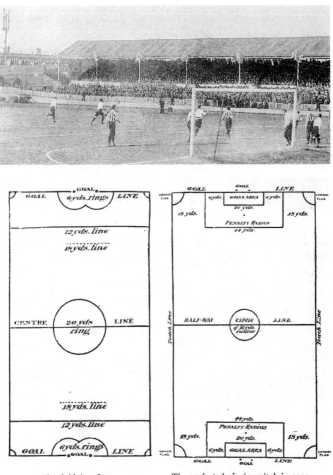

The field in 1892

The perfected playing pitch in 1905.

Top the old bra-shaped goal area at Bolton Wanderers' Ground, 1901
Above the original pitch layout of 1892 and perfected in 1905

127

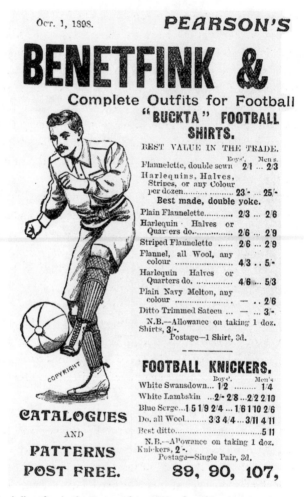

A football outfitter's advertisement from 1898 – flannelette shirts in stripes or harlequin halves and football 'knickers' in swansdown or lambskin

the two-handed throw-in became the rule. In 1891, the penalty kick was brought in for the first time, at the suggestion of the Irish FA, and a year later the practice of using umpires from each team to control football matches was abandoned, and neutral referees and linesmen were introduced. As *The Story of the Football League* puts it, "not only the description but the character of the office changed". Until then, the arrangements for the control of matches "were both primitive and inadequate, so much so that it was no uncommon thing for the officials to have to run the gauntlet of infuriated spectators in order to reach their quarters, and to be assaulted and pelted with anything that came to hand before they got there. Refereeing may have been more strenuous later, but it needed courage as well as competence to remain in it for long in the eighties and early nineties."[2] The Referees' Association was formed in 1893, no doubt in part to help their members practise their gauntlet-running, but also to fight for their match fees, which were often very late in coming. The changes the new rules and administration wrought were immediate. The average number of goals scored in the Football League in 1892–1893, the first season with both the penalty kick and neutral referees, fell below four goals a game for the first time.

By the end of the century, too, the success of the League and the acceptance of what one writer in 1895 called "the great blot on Association Football – professionalism" meant that a new industry was thriving but that in turn threw up new problems. Professionalism may have arrived, but that peculiarity of professional football, the transfer system, was not yet in place. The competition for the signatures of the best players was intense, with the inevitable result that many clubs were finding that their expenses exceeded their incomes, despite the undeniable fact that "thousands upon thousands of people pay their sixpences every Saturday of the season to witness a match".[3]

Clubs just tried to poach players when the opportunity arose. The League tried to stamp out this practice by fining clubs for fielding players they considered ineligible through lack of registration, but this became farcical after a while. J. Crabtree of Burnley, an England international, claimed that he was approached by several Aston Villa players on 13 April 1895 while playing with them for the English League against the Scottish League in Glasgow. The Villa players and their management denied any knowledge of the illegal approach, but Crabtree admitted that he wanted to move to Aston Villa and three months later he did, for a fee of three hundred pounds and the proceeds of a match at Burnley between the two clubs. No other action was taken against Aston Villa, nor against Crabtree who seemed to be more sinner than sinned against.

Player power was beginning to come into football, if something as basic as the right to play professionally for the club you want to play for can be reasonably described as "player power". Charles Alcock at the FA realised that professionals were not, as some had described them, "utter outcasts" but his was for some years a lone administrative voice crying in the wilderness. That was to be the difference between the 19th and the 20th centuries in professional sport: the 19th century belonged to the administrators, the 20th – eventually – to the players.

"A FINE DISREGARD FOR THE RULES"

There is a plaque on a stone set in the wall of the Close at Rugby School in Warwickshire which reads: "This stone commemorates the exploit of William Webb Ellis who, with a fine disregard for the rules of football as played in his time, first took the ball in his arms and ran with it, thus originating the distinctive feature of the Rugby game, AD 1823." The memorial stone was unveiled on 1 November 1923, one hundred years after the event it honours.

So that's easy; that's precisely how rugby football started, and where and when, end of story – or not. The story of William Webb Ellis picking up the ball and running with it is the cornerstone of rugby folklore, but there is little real proof of his 1823 heresy. We know that the game did begin at Rugby School, and that by the middle of the 19th century, it was developing very differently from what became soccer, but there is no clear evidence that Ellis did actually pick up the ball in a game of football at Rugby School, still less that this action would have shown "a fine disregard for the rules". Rugby football certainly grew out of the general free-for-alls around an inflated pig's bladder which was the primitive version of all codes of football, but the crucial role of William Webb Ellis in its birth is far less easy to confirm.

William Webb Ellis was born in 1807, so would have been sixteen years old when he committed the sort of foul that would have referees reaching for the red card these days. There is no doubt that he was a schoolboy at Rugby then, and it is possible that he played regularly in games of football at the school. Even before the arrival of Dr Arnold as headmaster in 1828, Rugby was a thriving school with many pupils regularly playing a variety of sports. But the problem comes when we consider the impact of what Ellis did. In 1823, there were no accepted rules of football, so it would have been difficult for him to show a fine disregard for them. Clearly, there were rules, or at least conventions, governing the way the game was played at Rugby at the time, but as "football" in those days covered all sorts of games involving any number of men or boys all trying to gain control of a ball, mainly but not exclusively by kicking it, it would be hard to say for sure that Ellis created havoc by picking the ball up, even if that was not allowed in the game played at Rugby. Even if he did, why did his action lead a large number of his schoolmates then and in later years to prefer his version of the game?

William Webb Ellis was described as a notable cricketer as a schoolboy, but also as a boy who "was inclined to take unfair advantage at football". The feature of his play that was deemed unfair was not that he "took the ball in his arms" but that he then ran with it. The rules at Rugby at the time, so we are led to believe, prohibited handling the ball unless it was in the air, in which case a player was allowed to catch it. At this point in the game, all players, including the catcher of the ball, were supposed to stay absolutely still. The catcher then had the option of either kicking the ball wherever he liked, or else of putting the ball on the ground and trying to kick it over the crossbar and between the posts of the goal. Nobody else was allowed to move until the kicker had moved closer to the goal than where he caught the ball. This makes the game sound rather like "grandmother's footsteps", the children's game where the players try to creep up on somebody while their back is turned, but anybody who is caught moving when the "grandmother" turns round is out. Perhaps Ellis thought the game was too childish in its present form, but whatever the reason, legend has it that he ran at the opposition with the ball in his hands. This was an extraordinarily foolhardy action; games in those days often involved up to three hundred players at any one time, and players taking the ball forwards were allowed to be tackled by the opposition, and then hacked (although it was not considered very fair to hold and hack at the same time). The sixteen-year-old William Webb Ellis might subsequently have worked out some tactics to go with his new approach to the game, but there is no evidence that he did so.

The legend also has it that after Ellis had picked up the ball and charged downfield with it in his hands, his captain apologised profusely to his opposite number for the breach of football etiquette. This seems exceedingly unlikely in an internal house match, if such it was. Remember, this was at a time when there were no referees and no set numbers of players per side. The possibility that a breach of etiquette would be noticed, let alone apologised for, seems little more than remote. The result of the game is unrecorded.

We have no idea whether William Webb Ellis himself thought any more about his afternoon's aberration, or whether any of his schoolmates did either. What we do know is that the rules of the game at Rugby School were not altered to take into account the idea of running with the ball until 1841, which was about fifteen years after Ellis had left the school, but significantly only two seasons after a large boy called Jem Mackie had followed Ellis's lead with some success. Mackie left Rugby in 1839. In 1846, *The Laws of Football as Played at Rugby School* were published, implying that the game had by this time gained some kind of national popularity.

Football at public schools in these days was generally frowned upon. Muscular Christianity did not take in brawling or hacking. Samuel Butler, headmaster of Shrewsbury until 1836, described football as "more fit for farm boys than young gentlemen", and an anonymous Old Etonian writing at the same time described it as "a game which the common people of Yorkshire are particularly partial to, the tips of their shoes being heavily shod with iron, and frequently death has been known to ensue". Schoolmasters, being *in loco parentis* during the school term, did not want too many dead bodies littered across their playing fields. The possibility of death from playing football was slightly less at Rugby than at many other schools, because they played on grass rather than paving stones. Still, the dangers would have been considerable, which is perhaps why the "everybody stand still after the ball has been caught" rule took effect.

Rugby did have one particular distinction that set it apart from other public schools of the time: there were far fewer sons of the aristocracy being educated there than at other public schools. When Dr Arnold arrived, he even went so far as to stop recruiting the offspring of noblemen as a matter of principle, so Rugby can fairly claim to have been a much more middle-class school than the other public schools of the day. So its version of football was a game developed by the sons of professional and businessmen of the middle classes, and thus cannot really lay

"Rugby Football at the Big Schools" – an article on the public school's game in
Boy's Own magazine c. 1918

claim to its famous description as a game for ruffians played by gentlemen. It is a game for ruffians played by ordinary people.

William Webb Ellis is forever remembered as the father of the game, but he has probably no more claim to that title than Walter Wingfield has to the title of "father of lawn tennis" or Abner Doubleday to be "father of baseball". Still, they all live on in the pantheon of sporting gods, because gods are matters of mythology, not fact. Ellis was the son of an officer in the Dragoons who was one of perhaps fifteen thousand soldiers killed at the Battle of Albuera on 16 May 1811, when William was only four years old. William came to Rugby in 1816, his mother having moved to Warwickshire after her husband's death because Rugby took talented pupils as Foundationer day boys free of charge, and William and his brothers qualified for this benefit. He went up to Brasenose College, Oxford, from Rugby in 1825, where he took part in the first-ever Oxford v Cambridge cricket match. (He made 12 batting at number three; the game was drawn "owing to the unfavourable state of the weather last Monday", as *Bell's Life* reported on 10 June 1827.) We do not know whether he played any games of football, and if so under which set of rules. He went on to take holy orders and was for some time the rector of St Clement Danes in the Strand in London, and then a country priest in Essex. He died on 24 January 1872, at the age of sixty-five, and is buried in Menton on the Mediterranean coast of France, between Monaco and the Italian border.

He would probably have been as surprised as anybody else to have been named the founding father of rugby football, but the main reason that he never entered the debate to settle things once and for all is that he had been dead for eight years before his unexpected nomination as the one true originator of the new code. It was another Old Rugbeian, Matthew Bloxam, writing in the school magazine *Meteor* in 1880, who put forward the idea that Ellis had been the first to pick up the ball and run. Bloxam was not just an Old Rugbeian at this time; he was a very Old Rugbeian. He had left the school four or five years before the 1823 incident he describes, which means that he would have been born around 1800 and was looking back at the age of eighty to an event of fifty-seven years earlier which he had only heard about second-hand at best. To be fair to Mr Bloxam as a source of accurate information, he was not only an Old Rugbeian but also the son of a schoolmaster there. His younger brother John was an exact contemporary of William Webb Ellis, and Matthew Bloxam was a noted local solicitor and local historian; he wrote one of the great worthy but dull books of his or any time – an eleven-volume work on Gothic architecture. So he was used to finding out and telling the truth. All the same, it seems that the story of William Webb Ellis became quite a crusade for him in his declining years, and it almost looks as though he had reached his verdict before sifting through all the evidence. There are no absolutely clear statements by anybody apart from Bloxam that it was William Webb Ellis in 1823 who took up the ball and ran with it in his arms.

The book that is the best source of the sporting life at Rugby at this time is a work as fictional as Matthew Bloxam's article, but certainly no less accurate in its account of Rugby life in the 1830s. It is *Tom Brown's Schooldays*, written by Thomas Hughes, who arrived at Rugby aged eleven in 1834. The book deals with many games of football, but never describes anybody running with the ball. A sub-committee of the Old Rugbeian Society was set up in 1895 to enquire into the origins of the game, and Hughes testified before this extraordinarily pompous

"Get up there – there's a little fellow under" — an illustration of the early game at
Rugby taken from *Tom Brown's Schooldays* by Thomas Hughes which was based
on his experiences under the headmastership of Thomas Arnold

sub-committee that running with the ball was unknown before his time. He wrote that "in my first year, 1834, running with the ball to get a try by touching down within goal was not absolutely forbidden, but a jury of Rugby boys of that day would almost certainly have found a verdict of 'justifiable homicide' if a boy had been killed in running-in." It was Hughes who brought the name of Jem Mackie into the argument, and he said that carrying the ball finally became legal when he was Captain of Big Side in 1841, Big Side being the field at the school where games were played. "Running-in," he wrote, "was made lawful within these limitations, that the ball must be caught on the bound, that the catcher was not off his side, that there should be no handing on, but that the catcher must carry the ball in and touch down".

Neither of the first two histories of the game, *History of Football for Five Centuries* by Montague Shearman in 1885 and *Football: The Rugby Union Game* by the bearded, cigar-smoking Reverend Frank Marshall in 1892, mentions Webb Ellis, but the sub-committee of the Old Rugbeians, anxious perhaps to secure for their alma mater the credit of inventing a major international sport, concluded that "at some time between 1820 and 1830, the innovation was introduced of running with the ball, and that this was in all probability done in the latter half of 1823 by Mr W. Webb Ellis". By 1900, it was accepted that Ellis had started the ball rolling; or not rolling, as the case may be.

Whether we care to believe the story of William Webb Ellis or not, it is obvious that his place is secure in the history of rugby football. It is equally obvious that there was no immediate switch from the kicking game to the handling game, at Rugby or anywhere else, as a result of what may or may not have happened on 1 November 1823. The changes really began to take place a decade or so later, when the young men who had played a handling game of football at Rugby School moved on to university. There they met the young men of Eton (who looked down with particular disdain on the middle-class students of Rugby), Charterhouse, Westminster, Winchester and several other schools, who all had different ideas of the way the game should be played.

Rugby's version of football was certainly famous by this time. In 1839, Queen Adelaide, the widow of King William IV who had died two years before, visited Rugby and made it clear that she wanted to see the boys playing football. Queen Adelaide, born Amelia Adelaide Louisa Theresa Caroline of Saxe-Meiningen in 1797, married the then Duke of Clarence in 1818, when there was a most indecorous rush to marry off the brothers of George IV so that an heir could be produced in due course. She proved to be a poor brood mare as none of her children survived infancy, so it was her niece by marriage, Queen Victoria, who inherited the throne when Adelaide's husband died. She had little in common with the remarkably fecund Queen Victoria, except perhaps that they both had parts of Australia named after them, and her interest in ball games was most unroyal. She spent some time on the touchline with Dr Arnold and his son, the poet Matthew Arnold, watching the boys play, many of them still wearing the tasselled velvet caps which had been specially made in commemoration of her visit. It must have been very difficult playing football while balancing a little skullcap on your head, but it was such a success that the caps became a regular part of a footballer's kit for many years, velvet tassel and all, and forms the basis of the design of the caps that would be awarded in later years to international rugby footballers.

The caps, rather oddly, became a standard part of every footballer's kit earlier than even boots, shirts or shorts. There is no evidence that special footwear had developed by the 1840s, although of course ordinary walking shoes were fearsome weapons on the feet of a well-built public schoolboy, and it was not until 1846 that Rugby school Big Side decided that "the parties at matches should be distinguished by the colours of their jerseys, the one party wearing white, the other striped jerseys". White trousers became standard at around this time, but they were knickerbockers buttoned below the knee rather than the football shorts we are used to these days.

The impetus that took the Rugby game into the outside world came almost exclusively from Old Rugbeians, firstly at university and then across the country. In 1839, the first university football club was founded, at Cambridge. The club was full of Old Etonians as well as Rugbeians, and the Etonians became rather irritated by the habit of the Rugbeians of picking up the ball and running with it – a clear hint that this was common practice at Rugby in the mid-1830s, even if it was still not officially within their rulebook. Something had to be done and, rather slowly, it was. On 28 August 1845, the first written rules were drawn up and approved by a committee of senior boys at Rugby school. There were thirty-seven rules in all, but their interest lies more in what they do not say than what they do.

Rule 27, for instance, stated that "no player but the first on his side may be hacked, except in a scrummage", but there was no definition of a scrummage. "No hacking with the heel, or above the knee, is fair", according to Rule 26, but there was no explanation of the size or shape of the playing area or the ball or the goals or the numbers of players on each side. At this time, players who had been awarded caps were allowed to take part in the main plays on Big Side, but the other boys had to stand in goal, as a kind of halfway house between goalkeepers and spectators. This created teams of perhaps two hundred boys on each side. Words like "offside", "knock-on" and "touch" all have their place in the 1845 rules, and the use of the hands is accepted from Rule 1: "A fair catch is a catch direct from the foot." The acceptance of the Ellis heresy comes in Rule 8: "Running-in is allowed to any player on his side [i.e. not offside] provided he does not take the ball off the ground, or take it through touch." The most alarming rule was Rule 20: "All matches are drawn after five days, but after three if no goal has been kicked." What is not recorded is how many hours each day the game was to continue, but the oranges at half-time must have been very welcome whenever they arrived.

These rules form the basis of what is now rugby football, but of course they were not acceptable to the Old Etonians at Cambridge. The Cambridge Rules were drawn up a year later, in 1846, and these specifically objected to hacking, running with the ball and scrummaging, three basic elements of the Rugby game. Still, somehow, the adherents of the two styles managed to play together for at least another fifteen years, and it was not until the 1860s that two quite distinct codes began to emerge.

The first rugby club to be founded beyond the school or the great universities was Guy's Hospital Rugby Football Club, which dates back to 1843. One of the first great football matches to take place outside either Rugby School or the universities, but which can still be described generally as rugby football, took place on 19 December 1857 at Edge Hill in Liverpool. The match was organised by the Gladstone family during a brief spell when William was out of the cabinet (and at the time

High Commissioner for the Ionian Islands), to show the moral superiority of football over hare coursing. The fact that the Gladstone family, locally and nationally highly influential, decided to promote the Rugby game rather than the Eton one which Gladstone, an Old Etonian, would have been familiar with, was due to the influence of Richard Sykes, who was at the time a guest of the Gladstones and a sixth-former at Rugby. The game was modestly billed as Rugby v The World. Its significance was probably as grandiose as that. It was Rugby versus the World from now on, the World being rather more inclined to the kicking game than the handling one. A new set of rules for football, known as the Sheffield Rules, had confirmed the Cambridge Rules' ban on hacking and handling in that same year, 1857, and this was confirmed in further rules drawn up in 1862.

When the Football Association was formed in 1863, one of the founder members was the Blackheath Football Club, which was a strong proponent of the rugby style of play. As a result of the Blackheath Club's persistence, it took the new Association six meetings to put together a set of rules for their version of the game. Blackheath wanted two specific rules included, to wit: "a player may be entitled to run with the ball towards his adversaries' goal if he makes a fair catch" and "if any player shall run with the ball towards his adversaries' goal, any player on the opposite side shall be at liberty to charge, hold, trip or hack him, or wrest the ball from him." The proposal by Blackheath to include these rules was defeated eventually by thirteen votes to four, and so Blackheath resigned from the Association.

If Blackheath had followed the example of the other three clubs who voted with them but did not resign from the Association, rugby football might have been strangled at birth,

England defeating Wales at Blackheath as depicted in the *London News* in 1892

but by resigning, they gave themselves the freedom to carry on playing the Rugby game, which thus survived to create its own Union. Blackheath was a very influential football club at the time, and if they had stayed in the Association, rugby football might have faded to become as obscure as the Eton Wall Game or a hundred other versions of local football around the world. Oddly, it was not the issue of handling the ball which was the breaking point for Blackheath. It was the issue of hacking – kicking opponents on the shins or tripping them as they ran – which the football players could not live with and Blackheath could not live without.

From 1863, association football, by organising itself, was able to gain a strong hold on the public imagination. Showing the confidence and the earnest desire to control the leisure hours of their inferiors that was the hallmark of the Victorian sporting reformers, Charles Alcock and his colleagues were establishing a lead for the association game which rugby needed to combat. That meant they, too, had to form an association, but to avoid confusion in the public's mind, they called it a union – the Rugby Football Union.

In December 1870, the secretary of the Richmond Football Club, Edwin Ash, wrote a letter to the newspapers proposing that "those who profess to play the Rugby game should meet to form a code of practice, as various clubs play to rules which differ from others, which makes the game difficult to play". With this piece of gentle understatement, Ash set in motion the chain of events which very quickly led to the formation of the Rugby Football Union. Barely a month later, on 26 January 1871, a meeting was held at the Pall Mall Restaurant in Cockspur Street in central London. Although the meeting was not held in the Star and Garter in Pall Mall, where the first meetings of the Jockey Club and the Marylebone Cricket Club had been held a century earlier, it is still remarkable that this part of London provided the restaurants which hosted the early organisational efforts of three major sports. There must have been something in the food that attracted sportsmen to the area.

At the Pall Mall Restaurant meeting, over twenty clubs and schools, including Blackheath Football Club, were represented. Without ever altering the way it played the game, Blackheath thus became a founder member of both the Football Association and the Rugby Football Union. What is more bizarre even than this is that when the rules for the rugby union game were finally agreed, the issue which had caused Blackheath to resign from the Football Association – hacking –

was outlawed by the Union as well. Blackheath men were not unfeeling thugs – their own rules in 1862 had been so enlightened as to outlaw throttling in the scrum – but their stand for the principle of breaking an opponent's shins had been to no avail. When Blackheath resigned from the Association, their representative, F.W. Campbell, had stated that without hacking, "you will do away with all the courage and pluck of the game, and I will be bound to bring over a lot of Frenchmen who could beat you with a week's practice". This was not a good prophecy. Despite the lack of hacking in either code, the first French victory in a rugby game against England in England did not come until 1951, and the first French victory against England in a soccer match in England has yet to occur. Clearly Mr Campbell overstated the importance of hacking in English international football dominance.

Things moved very quickly after the Pall Mall Restaurant meeting. A sub-committee was set up, as was the habit in those days, to formulate an agreed set of laws for the Rugby game. It consisted of three Old Rugbeians (who were very careful about preserving their hold on the game they had grown up with), who were also lawyers. One of them was Arthur G. Guillemard, a man whose influence on the infant code was enormous if not entirely beneficial. Guillemard and his colleagues created a code for the game, getting it written, read and agreed within six months of that first meeting.

The first laws of rugby football had fifty-nine separate clauses, covering all aspects of the game. Much of what was written is closely related to the rugby we know today, but there were one or two oddities. There were no points for tries, known then officially as "tries at goal", games being decided by the number of goals scored, the number of tries to count only if scores were otherwise level. The captains were to be the "sole arbiters of all disputes", even though at this stage referees were already becoming involved in association football, and the 1866 rules by then in use at Rugby School did include provision for umpires. The shape of the ball was not laid down, either. The ball had originally been a pig's bladder encased in leather panels, often cast-offs from a shoemaker stitched together to give the ball some durability. It was inflated by blowing through a clay pipe stem which was then capped to stop the air getting out again. In 1862, a rubber ball was patented, which enabled manufacturers to mould it precisely to any shape they wished, and this marked the beginnings of a clear distinction between the association football and the rugby football. But it was not until 1892 that the shape of the ball was written into the laws: from that time the ball had to be oval, between 25.5 and 26 inches in circumference at the middle and between 30 and 31 inches at the ends. In the early days, it was common enough for the balls also to have carrying handles, although contemporary pictures of the game being played do not seem to show the handle on the ball.

There was no set number of players per side in that first set of laws, although it seems to be accepted that the couple of hundred a side common at Rugby School was rather too much of a good thing. Twenty men on each side turned out when England played Scotland in the first-ever rugby international, at Raeburn Place, Edinburgh. The match was played on 27 March 1871, two months after the inaugural RFU meeting, but still three months before the code of laws was produced. Scotland, who at this time did not have its own Rugby Football Union, won by one goal and one try to one goal. The English team included Arthur Guillemard as one of the three backs (and ten

England against Scotland at the Oval in 1872

Old Rugbeians) in the English side. His own version of that first international game would have us believe that there were perhaps four thousand spectators present. This is almost certainly an exaggeration, but even two thousand people is a large crowd on a cold March day in Edinburgh to watch a new-fangled game which as yet had no agreed set of rules. Rugby was clearly taking hold of the public imagination.

The first rugby international in England was played on 5 February 1872 at the Kennington Oval, where the industrious Charles Alcock was trying to make sure that his ground was almost permanently in use. His description of the way the game was played shows how far it has developed since those infant days.

"Twenty a side formed the complement of a Rugby side ...and the play consisted largely of prolonged scrummages. They were the days of heavy forwards and, indeed, in this match the English twenty averaged 12st 8lbs per man, the Scotch a little over 12st."[1] The arrangement of an English team in the field, too, differed considerably from that of today (Alcock was writing this in 1904). Then the defence varied somewhat according to circumstance, consisting of two or occasionally three fullbacks, one three-quarter and two, sometimes three, half-backs.

Many of the players were equally good at other sports, including several cricketers and even one winter sports enthusiast, the three-quarter Harold Freeman, who helped develop the first toboggan run at Davos in 1879. But perhaps the most versatile was the Royal Engineer, Lt H.W. Renny Tailyour, playing for Scotland, who forty days later would play in the first-ever FA Cup final, also at The Oval. Renny Tailyour played in three finals in all, winning just once; he also played for Scotland against England in March 1873, yet again at The Oval, and scored a goal even though his side went down 4–2. He was an athletics Blue and "at his best a cricketer with very few superiors", playing county cricket for Kent sporadically throughout the 1870s. He provides yet another example of the Corinthian ideal so evident in the later years of Victoria's reign.

International rugby got underway quickly. The first soccer international, also England versus Scotland, did not happen until November 1872 – although there had been a series of "representative games" from 1870 – and the first cricket Test match was played in 1877. The Scottish Football Union, as it was known for the first fifty years of its existence, was formed in March 1873, the Irish Rugby Union in 1879 and the Welsh in 1881. All three nations were playing international football before they officially formed their Union, the Welsh having been beaten heavily by England in their first-ever international only three weeks before belatedly organising themselves, but it was the English Union that took the lead. It was, after all, the God-given right of the Victorian Englishman to organise and take charge of everything, from the Empire to a football match.

For the first decade and a half of organised rugby football, things went smoothly. The number of clubs affiliated to the English Union grew to well over four hundred, and Arthur Guillemard, first as honorary treasurer and secretary and then as president of the RFU from 1878 to 1882, watched with satisfaction as his sport flourished. Under him England, as the founder Union, made the laws and thus was solely responsible for the way the game was played and for arbitrating in any disputes which may have arisen. By 1878, the number of players per side had been fixed at fifteen; the Oxford v Cambridge match, beginning in 1872, had been between fifteens from 1875, and the first international fifteen-a-side match, England v Ireland, had taken place in 1877. The game was now beginning to be known as much for the skill of its backs as for the sheer brawn of its forwards and the length of the scrummages, which sometimes lasted for five minutes or more.

When the Calcutta Football Club disbanded in 1877, it handed over its remaining funds to the Rugby Football Union to create a cup which the Calcutta members wanted to be competed for on a knock-out basis between clubs in the same way as the FA Cup, which had proved so successful since its inauguration five years earlier. The eighteen-inch high Calcutta Cup which was thus created from the silver rupees left over in the Calcutta club's kitty was immediately recognised as one of the most elegant and exotic prizes in sport, with three king cobras as handles and a domed lid topped by an effigy of the Viceroy's own prize elephant, complete with a canopied howdah. But it was never used as a trophy for a knock-out competition between the member clubs of the RFU, probably because the men who ran it in London did not like the idea of a populist competition which would somehow detract from the social cachet the sport was rapidly acquiring. Despite Rugby's enviable reputation as a school unaffected by considerations of class or money – without which William Webb Ellis would never even have been accepted as a pupil – the Old Boys of the school who now formed the core of the RFU seemed to want to ally rugby to the establishment as quickly as possible, perhaps to distinguish it from its more proletarian cousin, soccer. Certainly, the desire to remain a truly amateur game in contrast to the professionalism creeping into golf, cricket and association football was a strong motivator for Arthur Guillemard and his fellow committeemen. So the Calcutta Cup was designated as the trophy for the winners of the annual England v Scotland match, a suitably elegant sporting and social occasion for this remarkable trophy to be associated with. The first Calcutta Cup match was in 1879.

The sixth match for the Calcutta Cup was almost the last. In 1884, England and Scotland fell into a dispute over the way a try appeared to have been scored: England said it was a try and Scotland said it was not. In the exchange of letters which followed the match, the English Union made the entirely fair point that as they made the laws, if they said it was a try, then a try it was. Oddly, this approach did not receive unanimous approval from the Scottish side of the border, and Scotland refused to play England in 1885. There were worrying signs that the men in charge at the RFU were beginning to lose absolute control over the game they had created.

In 1886, the Scottish, Irish and Welsh Unions joined together to form an International Board, but the English Union was reluctant to take part. The dispute rumbled on and in 1888 and 1889, the other Unions refused to play England. Eventually, the English Union was forced to climb down, and a compromise was reached whereby the English RFU joined the International Board, but with more representatives than the Celtic fringe nations. From 1886, these other Unions had forced home the idea that points should be awarded for tries as well as goals, and suddenly, it was no longer the English RFU's ball any more. If they went home in a huff, nobody would mind. Power was slipping through their fingers like a poor pass on a wet afternoon.

Rugby was spreading rapidly overseas at this time, and like football but unlike cricket, it was not only spreading among the colonies. There were the first glimmerings of interest in the game in France, and also reports of a game on 6 November 1869 at New Brunswick on the east coast of the United States, where Rutgers University beat Princeton. The match could not be described as exactly the same as rugby, but it was a rugby type of game, with twenty-five a side and played under Rutgers Rules, which were very like those in general use in England at the time. Rutgers won 6–4. A week later there was a return match, under Princeton Rules, which Princeton won, 8–0. Clearly, making up your own rules is something of which all 19th-century football players saw the advantage.

There is obviously something in the genes of rugby football that makes it mutate into slightly different variants, some of which spread with all the rapidity of a plague across the population infected, and some of which remain almost totally uncontagious, affecting only a small number of people among whom love for that particular variant is endemic. American football is one such mutant gene, which has all but entirely eliminated its parent on the American continent and is now battling with it on neutral territories for world domination. After the first rugby games in the 1870s in America, the lack of sensible rules began to frustrate the American players and spectators. In 1880, the American authorities (if there were any – the game was most popular at this time on the West Coast, never a place for strict codes of orthodox behaviour) unilaterally got rid of the scrum, replacing it with the "line of scrimmage". The game developed as the most popular winter ball game in most universities, but with its popularity went a high degree of brutality. By 1905, with eighteen deaths on the football field in America, President Theodore Roosevelt was forced to threaten to ban the sport altogether unless the footballers put their own house in order. As a direct result of this presidential intervention, in 1906 the forward pass was legalised and American football became a quite separate game from rugby.

Rugby was scarcely less violent back on home soil. Between January and March 1889, nine people died playing rugby, and in the three seasons from 1890 to 1893, seventy-one more people died playing rugby, with another three hundred and sixty-six people seriously injured. This was mass slaughter and it did nothing to make the game more popular in the public mind. It would be wrong to assume that this level of death and other damage was significantly worse per game than it had been in earlier years, because certainly there had been cases of boys being killed at Rugby School and at the universities. The game's brutality is also often cited as one of the reasons why it is so popular among medical students – it gives them plenty of opportunity to practise their newly learned skills in a real emergency. But as the game became more skilful and the players became more tactically aware, the way the game was being played was beginning to outgrow the original ideas of its founders. Control continued to slip away.

But the worst threat to the control of the RFU was not the safety of the sport, it was not the hybrid versions springing up in America, Australia and elsewhere, it was not even the upstart Scots, Irish and Welsh imagining that they should have a say in the way the game was run. It was the upstart northern clubs, who seemed quite happy to take on cobblers, window cleaners and factory workers as players and, even worse, as members with full voting rights, who represented the real threat to the rugby establishment. It was no coincidence that the efforts to establish the credentials of William Webb Ellis as the true originator of the sport should be going on at exactly the same time as the northern clubs were threatening to split away from the Union. Their reasons for wanting to secede were the oldest and most demeaning of all: money. In 1895, professionalism was rearing its ugly, not to say utterly uncouth, head and the only way the establishment could see to combat it was by establishing the truth and purity of the Union game, as represented by the innocent schoolboy, Oxford scholar and Church of England priest William Webb Ellis – the only true begetter of the game.

Association football almost split in two over the issue of money, but at the end of the day we have to give credit to the lads for drawing back from the edge of that particular precipice. Rugby football, having been born from the desire of Blackheath men to continue hacking, was less worried about a further fractionalisation, and the arguments which developed between North and South, between the rulers and the masses, between

the Gentlemen and the Players, proved beyond hope of compromise. A typical example of the northern clubs was the one
founded at Rochdale, the cradle of the Cooperative Movement,
in 1867. The founding members of the club included the local
lord of the manor, a magistrate, a pub keeper and a tobacconist.
Once the club began playing matches the next year, its players
included working men playing with the tradesmen and the
landed gentry. This club was called the Rochdale Hornets, and
from the very beginning they charged admission to their games.
At Wigan, just down the road, they played on common land,
and could only pass collection boxes round for voluntary dona-
tions from the spectators.

The clubs paid their players, too. There was little prevari-
cation about this, and most clubs admitted more or less openly
that they paid "broken-time" payments to the working men in
their teams. At a time when the average industrial wage was
around twenty-seven shillings (£1.35) for a fifty-six and a half
hour week, a man could not afford to take time off unpaid to
play any sport. So the clubs paid their men at the going rate for
the hours they put in at the club when otherwise they could have
been earning. If rugby wanted to compete with football, where
professionalism had been allowed, at the very least they had to
concede the principle of these broken-time payments, or so the
northern clubs began to argue. How else could the working
man compete with the idle rich or the self-employed?

Soon matters went beyond mere broken-time payments.
Dickie Lockwood, who played for Dewsbury and England, was
rumoured to earn only nine shillings a week as a printer in the
wool industry, but he earned a further ten shillings from
Dewsbury, quite apart from a one-pound appearance fee every
time he played in an exhibition match. Not surprisingly, he

played in many exhibition matches. Testimonial funds were established by clubs for their best players, and in other clubs it was soon discovered that several of the best players worked for companies owned or run by leading committee members of the same club. All of this was a red rag to the bull of the RFU in London, who continued to trumpet the virtues of the noble amateur against the pernicious professional, who played for personal glory and wealth and not merely for the love of the game. The northern professionals saw rugby as a way out of their terrible social predicament, for themselves and their families. The wealthy aristocrats of the Rugby Football Union wanted nothing more than to remain in their splendid social framework, themselves and their families, for as long as they could. Somebody's applecart was bound to be upset.

In 1886, the RFU drew up a definition of a professional, and issued it to all member clubs. A professional was, in their view:

a) Any player who shall receive from his club or any member of it, any money consideration whatever, actual or prospective, for services rendered to the club of which he is a member. Note – This sub-section is to include any money considerations, paid or given to any playing member, whether as secretary, treasurer or other officer of the club, or for work or labour of any sort done on or about the ground or in connection with the club's affairs.

This sub-section ruled out the little trick that county cricket clubs were beginning to devise, whereby leading but impoverished amateur players would be appointed as secretary or to some other lesser club position, without jeopardising their amateur status on the field. But the RFU had not finished their definition yet. They ploughed ruthlessly on:

b) Any player who receives any compensation for loss of time, from his club or any member of it. c) Any player trained at the club's expense, or at the expense of any member of the club. d) Any player who transfers his services from one club to another on the consideration of any contract, engagement or promise on the part of a club, or any member of that club, to find him employment. e) Any player who receives from his club, or any member of it, any sum in excess of the amount actually disbursed by him on account of hotel or travelling expenses incurred in connection with the club's affairs.

And anyone else who knows me. This was a catch-all definition which was almost certain to lead to the break-up of the Union, because so much was unprovable and geared towards the breeding of suspicion. If a player moved his work and in so doing switched his allegiance to another club, who was to say that was a genuine move or that he was a professional under sub-section d)? If, like the Leeds Parish Church club, there was an odd entry in the books, who was to be sure that it did not cover genuine expenses rather than the cost of a champagne and oyster supper and a cruise on the River Mersey for the whole team while fulfilling an away fixture? The Reverend Frank Marshall, that's who. Mr Marshall, a headmaster and leading member of the Yorkshire RFU who has already slipped into the narrative as author of one of the earliest histories of the game, was the Savonarola of the RFU, with all of the Florentine's zealous enthusiasm but none of his immediate popularity among the oppressed classes.

Marshall thought the RFU definition of professionalism did not go nearly far enough, but he used it as his gospel to great effect. Over the next few seasons, he was responsible for swingeing punishments being brought against several teams, including Brighouse Rangers, Leeds St John's, Leeds Parish Church, Heckmondwike, Wakefield Trinity and even his own club, Huddersfield, against whom he testified because they had induced two players to join them from Cumberland. Matters came to a head on 20 September 1893, at a general meeting of the RFU at the Westminster Palace Hotel in London, attended by four hundred and thirty-one delegates, some of whom were rather late in arriving as they managed to get lost on unfamiliar territory between King's Cross station and the hotel. The motion tabled by the northern faction was that "players be allowed compensation for *bona fide* loss of time", but they made too many tactical errors even before the meeting was underway to hope to win the day. The RFU made sure that there were men of the right persuasion to vote as proxies for any northern club that could not come, and they also made sure that Oxford and Cambridge Universities, bulwarks of amateurism, had twenty-nine votes between them.

The arguments were, to our ears, very one-sided. The "professionals" were bound to win. The proposer of the motion, James Miller, asked whether it was reasonable that "the working man has to leave his work and lose his wages to play for the benefit of his club, his county or his country, but he receives no recompense for his loss of wages." The nub of the question was, "Why should they take part in matches at a loss to themselves?" The RFU response, from the RFU secretary, G. Rowland Hill, was so condescending to the players that it almost beggars belief.

"What this means is paying men for playing football. What will be the effect on the working man?" He went on to suggest that, "a man might be away a whole week, and thus earn his wages without doing a single stroke of work", entirely forgetting that it was in effect what all the amateurs of the day did anyway.

They lived on unearned income "without doing a single stroke of work" not just for a whole week, but for a whole lifetime. Somehow that was not a moral problem, whereas paying a man to work hard on the rugby field for his club, his county or his country was.

It requires no great analytical or forecasting skills to guess that the RFU carried the day. But they did not just win the debate and attempt to heal wounds. They won the day and immediately ordered a Special General Meeting that same night which changed the RFU's composition so that "only clubs composed entirely of amateurs shall be eligible for membership, and its headquarters shall be in London where all general meetings shall be held". So take that, you uncouth northerners. Don't you dare rattle our cage again.

The northern clubs took two more years to make the final break, but on 29 August 1895, a meeting was held at the George Hotel, Huddersfield, from 6.30 p.m. That Thursday evening twenty-one delegates gathered, representing leading clubs in Yorkshire and Lancashire. They quickly passed the main proposal of the night, "that the clubs here represented decide to form a Northern Rugby Football Union and pledge themselves to push forward without delay its establishment on the principle of payment of *bona fide* broken time only". The clubs then submitted their resignations from the RFU (all except Dewsbury, who had cold feet at the last minute) and rugby league was born.

The struggle by the amateur establishment against the incoming tide of professionalism seems to us, a hundred years on, to be nothing more than a pale imitation of King Canute. But the principles of *mens sana in corpore sano*, of muscular Christianity and of the fundamental soundness of the class system were deeply held and the leaders of the Rugby Football Union had no way of knowing that professional rugby would one day be the norm, nor indeed that their uncontested position at the top of the social tree would crumble two decades later in the mud not of any rugby pitch, but of the Somme. Amateurism took far longer to die than the average lieutenant in the Great War.

"The ancient game of tennis"

The story of lawn tennis is a remarkable one. It was the last but one major team sport in Britain (rugby union being the last) to admit that professionals exist, but its origins were founded in pure commercial opportunism. Its development as a major international sport had nothing to do with the proper education of young men or colonial ideals or even, in the end, financial gain, but its initial popularity was seen as a commercial opportunity, eagerly seized and exploited. It was upper-middle class commercial opportunism rather than proletarian money grabbing, but it was commercial opportunism all the same. The game of tennis known these days as real or royal tennis, is the clear ancestor of the game, but that version had the major disadvantage of having to be played in a vast and very costly indoor court, which meant inevitably that there were few courts and those that existed were almost entirely owned, and played on, by the landed gentry. Royal tennis was not a game for the masses.

It was still an energetic game. Samuel Pepys records in his diary that King Charles II used to play real tennis. Pepys was present one morning when "the King, playing at tennis, had a steelyard carried to him; and I was told it was to weigh him after he had done playing; and at noon Mr Ashburnham told me that it is only the King's curiosity, which he usually hath of weighing himself before and after his play, to see how much he loses in weight by playing; and this day he lost four and a half pounds." This was indeed a tough game, made even tougher if played in its original form, as a *jeu de paume* – a game played with the palm of the hand rather than with a racket. Fives, as well as lawn tennis and squash, descends directly from real tennis.

The name "tennis" is one shrouded in debate. The most common explanation is that it derives from the French *tenez!*, meaning "hold!" or "watch out!", the cry of the server to his opponent. Another possible derivation is from the ancient Egyptian town of Tamis or Tinnis, where they made the linen that was used to make the earliest balls. Some say it comes from "tens", being double the quantity of "fives" to which it is clearly related. Perhaps it comes from the German *tanz*, although there is no evidence of such a game being played in Central Europe before Baron Gottfried von Cramm in the 1930s. All we can say for certain (or for reasonably certain) is that real tennis is a French game in origin.

There was a version of tennis that became, briefly, a game with a greater appeal among the less reputable classes. Rackets was a game that evolved from tennis in the unlikely setting of the English prison system, most notably the debtors' prison, the Fleet. The debtors' prisons often contained well-educated and originally wealthy men who had played real tennis before their incarceration, and saw the value of playing such a game to keep body and mind fit in otherwise very unhygienic conditions. But they could not build their own real tennis courts in prison, so they had to make do with the next best thing – the prison courtyard. In 1820, the first generally acknowledged champion of rackets was one Robert Mackay, described as "a debtor of unsavoury reputation", who learned the game in prison, and the game is described in some detail in Dickens's *Pickwick Papers*, written in 1836 and 1837. When Mr Pickwick finds himself inside the Fleet Prison for refusing to pay the damages and costs awarded against him in the breach of promise case brought by Mrs Bardell, Pickwick's landlady, he comes across fellow inmates playing rackets. Mr Pickwick does not play rackets, but he cannot avoid seeing it played.

"The area formed by the wall in that part of the Fleet in which Mr Pickwick stood was just wide enough to make a good racket court; one side being formed, of course, by the wall itself and the other by that portion of the prison which looked (or rather would have looked, but for the wall) towards St Paul's Cathedral."

This was the court on which they played, and Pickwick was just one of many spectators "sauntering or sitting about, in every possible attitude of listless idleness". There were also free men outside the prison who climbed up to the windows "looking on at the racket players, or watching boys as they cried game". Pierce Egan's *Book of Sports*, written in 1832, describes rackets as "one of the most healthful exercises connected with British sports, and the principal Amusement for confined debtors in the Fleet and King's Bench Prisons".

He goes on to mention a "man of the name of Hoskins, who was at one period of his confinement the racket-master, a capital player, and who altered the game from 11 to 15" (i.e. he changed the number of points required to win a game from eleven to fifteen). Hoskins was effectively the resident professional in the King's Bench Prison, "waiting upon gentlemen with the bats and balls, and frequently taking a hand in the match, he was enabled to support his family of seven children".

Mixed doubles at the country manor from the *Girl's Own* paper, 1883.
Tennis grew out of the Victorian world of garden games like croquet

Hoskins was obviously an eccentric, like most of the great sportsmen of his era. Egan tells us that he was a well-born Cornishman: "His father was a respectable surgeon and Hoskins was brought up a gentleman; he was here at the suit of a single creditor, one whom he once called friend and benefactor, and for a disputed debt which he vowed he would never pay." Hoskins died in December 1823, "after an uninterrupted imprisonment of thirty-eight years". This could well be the longest imprisonment ever suffered by a professional sportsman in history.

Perhaps understandably, given the reputation of the public schools at the time, the game spread quickly from the prisons to the leading schools, but it was not until 1862, when William (later Sir William) Hart-Dyke, an Old Harrovian, won the national title that the holder of the championship was somebody who had not learnt the game in prison. He was also the first amateur to win the title; the connection in the public mind between professionalism and criminality was not difficult to make in those days.

Lawn tennis was a product of that most amateur and middle class of institutions, the vicarage tea party. It was conceived during those long sultry English summer days in suburban gardens, and was born at a Christmas gathering on the Welsh border. The popularity of croquet, a ball game in which the ladies were allowed to take part because it could be played without raising any perspiration or hemlines, had resulted in regular social gatherings in those elegant Victorian gardens which had a flat lawn large enough to accommodate hoops and pegs. It had also made the younger generation aware of the joys of mixed sporting competition, and croquet quickly became part of the upper-middle-class courting ritual. But how much better might a courtship go if the game played were a little more energetic?

The croquet lawn was the first necessity for lawn tennis. Croquet is yet another ball game with obscure origins, but is clearly related to other stick and ball games, including golf, cricket and hockey. Although there had been recognisable versions of the game played for at least two centuries in England, it burst upon Victorian society in the 1850s, thanks in part to the work of a sporting goods manufacturer, John Jaques of Hatton Garden, who not only manufactured the sets, including mallets, hoops and balls, but also wrote a book about the game. He was as uncertain as anybody about where the game actually came from, admitting that, "the history of croquet is peculiar. It found its way into the world without any acknowledged parentage, and immediately won a popularity which has almost revolutionised an outdoor social life." His views were echoed by an anonymous poet, who like all sporting poets of almost any age, lapses into doggerel at the first opportunity. In this case, the bard of croquet wisely hid his (or her) identity:

> Whence croquet sprang to benefit the earth,
> What happy garden gave the pastime birth,
> What cunning craftsman carved its graceful tools,
> Whose oral teachings fixed its equal rules?
> Sing Jaques, then apostle of the game.

As if those lines were not enough, the poet returns to the theme a line or two later, and in so doing challenges strongly for the right to claim the weakest couplet ever written about any sport anywhere:

> Mysterious croquet! like my "Little Star"
> Of infancy, "I wonder what you are?"

By the 1860s, lawns which had previously played host to nothing more strenuous or more precise than picnics and games of bowls were made much more level and much more open. Shrubs, bushes and trees were transplanted, the grass was cut, the moss was removed and the surface became harder with regular rolling. The lawns were made ready for croquet.

They were also, although their owners did not know this in the 1860s, ready for lawn tennis. The invention of the game is at the same time absolutely clear and shrouded in uncertainty. We are certain that on 23 February 1874, Major Walter Clopton Wingfield entered a patent application for his "New and Improved Portable Court for Playing the Ancient Game of Tennis". However, uncertainty is introduced into the issue when we realise that Major Wingfield's patent application (which was for the portable court, not the entire game) came two years after the first lawn tennis club had been established. The Leamington Lawn Tennis Club dates from 1872, having

Major Wingfield, 'inventor' of lawn tennis

been founded by another army man, Major T.H. Gem.

Major Walter Clopton Wingfield was an interesting, if rather pompous, man. He was born on 16 October 1833, of an exceedingly ancient family, whose seat was Rhysnant Hall in Montgomeryshire. Major Wingfield's entry in *Who's Who* made the point that "the Wingfields are one of the oldest families in England, as they were located at Wingfield Castle in Suffolk when William the Conqueror came over." One of his ancestors, John Wingfield, had been gaoler to Charles of Orleans, grandson of Charles VI of France, known as both "the Mad" and "the Well-Beloved", the former presumably when he was out of earshot, the latter to his face. Charles of Orleans had been captured at Agincourt, and was known as an enthusiastic real tennis player, and it seems likely that Walter Wingfield's obsession with his ancestry may well have stirred the initial interest in tennis and set the spark that led eventually to his invention of a whole new ball game.

Wingfield had served with the King's Dragoon Guards in China and had married, in 1858, Miss Alice Cleveland, daughter of an army general. He retired from the army in 1861 with the rank of major, and began experimenting with a game that was influenced by badminton, a game that he had observed in India. In 1869, he tried out the game with three of his friends, whose influence would prove to be crucial in the future spread of the game. The three young men were, firstly, Henry Charles Keith Fitzmaurice, the fifth Lord Lansdowne, then aged twenty-four, later to become Governor-General of Canada and then Viceroy of India; secondly, a man who had been Lansdowne's fag at Eton, the future Conservative prime minister Arthur Balfour, then aged twenty-one; and thirdly, Walter Long, who was then only fifteen years old and a schoolboy at Harrow, but who would go on to become a minister in Balfour's government and in 1921, the first Viscount Long. The influence of Harrovians on lawn tennis began that day, and continued for many years to come. As a result of their gentle games on the lawn of Lord Lansdowne's London house in Berkeley Square, Wingfield devised simple instructions and the layout for a game to be called lawn tennis.

Well, at first it was not going to be called lawn tennis, it would be called "sphairistike", a word derived rather pompously from the Greek *sphairos* meaning a ball. The name was no doubt thought up to distinguish Wingfield's game from all the other versions of lawn tennis which were being played during the 1860s and 1870s, and it certainly achieved that aim. But, according to Lord Lansdowne's own memoirs, he told Wingfield that the name sphairistike would not work. Walter Long, no doubt suffering from the benefits of a classical Harrovian education, said that the name was far too difficult to remember, let alone spell, and it was apparently Balfour's idea to call the game lawn tennis. Balfour, as a future politician (he was first elected to Parliament in 1874), was no doubt already practising the art of claiming for himself another person's good idea, because there is little doubt that he did not make up the name; he merely appropriated a name that was already in the public domain.

At this point we revert to Major T.H. Gem. Harry Gem was a retired army man, clerk to the Birmingham magistrates. He played an outdoor version of tennis in his garden in Edgbaston, that fashionable part of Birmingham now more famous for its cricket ground as well as for its annual ladies tennis championships. Gem and his friend J.B. Perera had played their game, which they first called *pelota*, after the Basque racket sport, and then "lawn rackets", from the 1860s, a time when there are also records of a similar game being played as far apart as Roxburghshire and Suffolk. They developed the game as a doubles event with the help of two local doctors as playing partners at the Manor House Hotel, Leamington Spa, and in 1872, they formed the Leamington Lawn Tennis Club. The club then published its *Rules of Lawn Tennis*.

Sphairiotikon or The Major's Game, precursor of modern
Lawn Tennis as illustrated in Wingfield's *Book of Games*, 1873

Major Gem's activities all pre-dated Wingfield's invention of sphairistike, which he tried out in its final form at a Christmas party at Nantclwyd in 1873. Wingfield's idea at this stage was that the game was ideal not as a summer sport as Gem had envisaged it, but as an activity for clear winter days when the ground was too frosty for hunting. The lawn was not a crucial part of the game, and there is no evidence that the inventor saw his game as anything other than a bracing winter activity. Wingfield had published his *Book of Games* in 1873, and in it had described the erection of a net across a court and outlined the rules on how to play his game. The application for a patent two months after his Christmas party shows how much the game had been enjoyed by the holidaymakers at Nantclwyd, but the patent application was actually for the "new and improved portable court for the playing of the ancient game of tennis", rather than for the game itself. As one historian notes, "he was persuaded to market it",[1] although all we know about Major Wingfield leads us to believe that he did not require much persuasion. His marketing involved the creation of a kit in the style of John Jaques the croquet kit maker, which included pegs, poles, nets and a mallet to bang the poles into the ground, all for five guineas. What the kit did not include was either rackets or balls, because Wingfield assumed people would use real tennis rackets and the comparatively new India rubber balls, developed as a result of the American Charles Goodyear's invention of the vulcanisation process in 1839.

In the longer run, the equipment needed to succeed at lawn tennis proved to be quite different. Wilfred Baddeley, three times Wimbledon champion in the 1890s, believed that "the first thing that a man who intends to take up lawn tennis as a pastime should look to is the purchase of really good implements wherewith to play."[2] Although Baddeley did not give any specific advice on the implements wherewith to play, he did go on to say that, "unless this is done, he may find that, despite his practice, not the slightest improvement seems to be made, and naturally he will soon get disgusted with himself and the game".

The main piece of equipment required is, of course, the racket. Wingfield's assumption that real tennis rackets would be suitable for the lawn variety soon proved to be wrong. The lop-sided rackets were entirely unsuited to the new game but it was not until the mid-1880s, up to eight years after the Wimbledon Championships had begun, that a tennis racket with a round or oval head became the norm. Until around 1880, they were as likely to be called "bats" as rackets, and at first every maker of the things, whatever they were known as, had his own ideas of what they should look like.They were generally made of one piece of ash wood steam-bent into shape and strung either with cat gut or, originally, with wire. They cost anything from one guinea to thirty shillings (£1.05 to £1.50), which was a significant sum of money for a piece of sporting equipment in those days, and another reason why the sport has retained its middle-class image for so long.

With the purpose-made lawn-tennis rackets of the 1880s, the balls could be hit hard and accurately, and the pat-a-cake version of tennis invented by Wingfield was dealt a mortal blow. The ball to be used was also crucial to the growth of the sport. Early organisers and players soon discarded Wingfield's idea of a solid ball in the real tennis or rackets style, and came to favour the now entirely familiar hollow rubber ball, covered in flannel, which was adopted officially by 1876. This was the final element which gave lawn tennis its pace. With rackets that could hit the ball hard and accurately, and a ball that flew con-

172

Anyone for tennis? – the relatively expensive cost of the racket and the
exclusivity of the clubs helped keep tennis a middle-class pursuit

sistently through the air and bounced consistently off the grass,
the game became one of the fastest of racket sports, even if
nobody was serving at 200 kph as is not uncommon a hundred
years later. In due course, the implements used to play the game

also ensured the death of sphairistike, because they were not compatible with the court and net layout, and something had to give. Wingfield's decision not to include rackets and balls in his kits was to prove fatal to the prospects of sphairistike but exactly right for the growth of its bastard son, lawn tennis.

Despite its shortcomings, the success of Wingfield's kit was immediate and astonishing. He managed to gain for his game – and more importantly, for the playing sets at five guineas a time – editorial recommendations in a number of publications, most significantly *The Army and Navy Gazette*, for it was thanks to its immediate and enthusiastic adoption by the armed forces as a source of energetic and easily transportable recreation that it spread overseas almost as rapidly as it did in Britain. It was as instant a success as any leisure phenomenon one can think of, from the hula hoop to Rubik's cube to skateboarding, despite the lack of any national communications media more effective than the newspapers and magazines of the day. The really surprising thing was that it did not prove to be an overnight craze but a lasting and lucrative sport.

The game arrived in the United States in 1875, introduced by Miss Mary Outerbridge, who had spent the winter of 1874 in Bermuda and had seen the British army garrison playing Major Wingfield's game there, just one year on from his Nantclwyd Christmas party. She took a lawn-tennis set, complete with rackets and balls obtained from the regimental stores, back with her to New York, where her brother, who gloried in the name of A. Emilius Outerbridge, helped her lay out a court at the Staten Island Cricket and Baseball Club.

Between July 1874 and July 1875, over one thousand sphairistike kits were sold in Britain, mainly to the upper classes, who were, of course, the only people with the space, the time and the money to partake in this new sport. Major Wingfield was also helped initially by the chaos and bitterness which was engulfing the world of croquet, which would in the longer term have very positive repercussions on the game of lawn tennis, but rather more negative ones on Major Wingfield's bank balance.

The general belief seems to be that it was Wingfield's book and the patent that established tennis as the major sport it is today, but there is much more to the story than this. The initial spread of the sport undoubtedly owed everything to Wingfield's sphairistike kits and his well-born friends and connections: even the Prince of Wales and the future Tsar Nicholas II of Russia acquired sets. But within three years, Wingfield's patent had lapsed and the game of lawn tennis that was being played on vicarage lawns and, for the first time, at Worple Road, Wimbledon, was a significantly different game from the one Wingfield described in his book.

The game of croquet was torn apart in the late 1860s and early 1870s by a dispute involving Walter Jones Whitmore, the man who first devised rules for the game and wrote *The Science of Croquet*, published in 1866. In 1867, Whitmore organised the first National Croquet Championship at Evesham, which he won; at this time, the croquet craze was in full flow. In 1868, a proposal was put forward to create an All England Croquet Club, under the chairmanship of J.H. Walsh, the editor of the influential sporting magazine *The Field*. Whitmore was elected honorary secretary. But before long, the highly opinionated and argumentative Whitmore had fallen out with Walsh, and Whitmore was sacked. His reaction was to set up a rival croquet club, the National Croquet Club, with the result that in 1869 there were two national championships and a great deal of bitterness in the newspaper columns of the time. All publicity is good publicity, they say, but the antics of the two croquet clubs in 1869 went some way towards disproving this theory.

In 1871, Walsh's All England Croquet Club bought land at Worple Road, Wimbledon, as a headquarters for their club. Whitmore, certainly not one of the more affable members of mid-Victorian sporting society, fell out with many of his National Croquet members, who thereupon switched their allegiance to the All England. This merely prompted Whitmore to rename his club the Grand National Croquet Club. He was still fighting his corner when he died suddenly in 1872, and by then the damage to the popularity of croquet was almost as terminal as Whitmore's fate. The Grand National Croquet Club faded away with Whitmore's death and the All England Croquet Club fell upon very hard times. It was only when members of the All England Croquet Club saw the advantage of turning over some of their land to the new game of lawn tennis that their future began to look brighter, even though it was an entirely different future from the one they had originally planned.

One of J.H. Walsh's closest associates at *The Field*, and an authority on all indoor sports, was Dr Henry Jones, born in London on 2 November 1831. Jones had given up medicine at the early age of twenty-five (it was hardly worth his while qualifying, for he scarcely practised medicine, but he was in a way a forerunner of the most famous sporting doctor of Victorian times, Dr W.G. Grace) to become a full-time sports writer, using the pen-name "Cavendish". Jones was a member of the committee of Walsh's All England Croquet Club, and it was he who first saw the opportunities presented to them by the sudden rise of lawn tennis. On 25 February 1875, just one year and two days after Wingfield had applied for his patent, a motion was proposed at the one hundred and fourth committee meeting of the All England Club "that one ground be set apart for lawn tennis and badminton during the ensuing season". The proposer was Dr Henry Jones, and the motion was duly carried.

Another key figure in the development of lawn tennis is J.H. Hale, the captain of Sussex County Cricket Club from 1863 to 1866. Hale, born on 16 September 1830, was a big-hitting opening batsman and leader of a team that included John Wisden, who founded the *Cricketers' Almanack* that still bears his name, and Spencer Austen-Leigh, grand-nephew of Jane Austen. Austen-Leigh achieved the remarkable feat, when playing for Sussex against Kent in 1862, of being one of four victims in consecutive balls from the bowling of "Tiny" Joseph Wells, the five foot two inch professional cricketer and father of H.G. Wells. This is the only known direct sporting link between *Pride and Prejudice* and *The War of the Worlds*.

Hale, like so many other Victorian gentleman sportsmen, spread his interests across many sports, and on his retirement from cricket became closely involved in the development of croquet as a founder member of Walsh's All England Club. Along with Walsh and the prickly Walter Jones Whitmore, he became one of the first three life members of the club in 1868, although for him, the life membership proved to be ten years (six years longer than Whitmore's). He then became interested in lawn tennis, and developed his own "Germains Lawn Tennis" but this did not catch on, despite having a rectangular court, which was much more suited to an athletic sport. Sphairistike, the social pastime, ruled the day. However, the variety of different versions of the game being played, from the Leamington version championed by Major Gem, to the Wingfield and Hale games as well as several other minor varieties led to a desire to establish a general set of rules as quickly as possible.

The Field had begun the debate on the way lawn tennis should be played as early as their edition of 21 March 1874, just four weeks after Wingfield's patent application. For the next fifteen months or so, the debate raged in their columns and elsewhere. No final decision was reached until a few weeks before the first All England lawn-tennis championships in 1877. Major Wingfield's game had several features which were not to last for long, notably the hourglass shape of the court, so that it was narrower at the net than at the baselines, and the height of the net, which was at least four feet at the centre and five feet high at the posts. Wingfield's game was a social pat-ball game; what the All England Club was creating, under the energetic drive of Dr Henry Jones, was a vigorous international sport.

The final arbiter of the rules ought to have been the Marylebone Cricket Club. It was logical that the All England Club should turn to MCC as the authority on the rules, as they were the arbiters of both real tennis and rackets, the games from which the new game was most obviously descended. Under the guidance of J.M. Heathcote, who was to win the Golden Racquet for real tennis at Lord's every year between 1867 and 1881, MCC had installed a lawn tennis court in 1874, a decision that was furiously attacked at the club's AGM on 5 May 1875 but which Heathcote defended with the opinion that lawn tennis was "an athletic and popular game". After trying out both Wingfield's and Hale's versions of the game, MCC duly issued a code of laws on 29 May 1875, and less than a month later, the All England Club adopted them as the rules they would play to. This proved to be a very short-lived and unpopular decision. The MCC laws, for the game they called lawn tennis, adopted Major Wingfield's hourglass shape of the court, his high-sided sagging net and his scoring system, based on the rackets system in which only the server could score points. This was good news for sales of his five-guinea sphairistike sets.

In 1877, two years after the MCC laws had been adopted, the All England Croquet Club changed its name officially to the All England Croquet and Lawn Tennis Club, and it was decided at a committee meeting on 2 June that year that "a public meeting be held on July 10th and following days to compete for the Championships in lawn tennis". The example already being shown by golf, association football and cricket in creating a method of finding out who was the best in the land was eagerly followed by the tennis authorities, although they only gave themselves thirty-eight days to get ready. A sub-committee was set up to look at the rules under which it would be played.

Remarkably, it was at this point that the rules drawn up by MCC were in certain crucial respects abandoned. The sub-committee decreed on 16 June, with only twenty-four days to go before their first championship, that the hourglass shape of the court – the key element in Wingfield's game – should be abandoned, and also that "each match will be the best of five sets, without advantage sets except in the final tie". This was the first time that any lawn-tennis event would be played with the now standard method of tennis scoring. Until now, lawn tennis had generally used the rackets method of scoring, as recommended by both Wingfield and Hale, but changes had been advocated in the columns of *The Field* since the previous year. Every battle seems to have been waged in the columns of *The Field*, still edited by the honorary secretary of the All England Club, J.H. Walsh, and still giving space to its controversial columnist "Cavendish", Henry Jones. It was Jones who was most insistent that changes should be made to the scoring system, and as he was a key member of the championship sub-committee, he got his way. From now on, the receiver could score points as well as the server. No longer was the winner the first to fifteen points. Each game became a battle over four points, and each set went to the first to win six games. The extraordinary excitement and tension of the swings from near defeat to ultimate victory within a few games which are now a trademark of lawn tennis began with Henry Jones's determination to get his way in 1877. Also in that year, Major Wingfield's patent application lapsed, and sphairistike, or "sticky" as it had come to be known, faded into the sunset.

There is no logical reason why the scoring of tennis is the way it is. Why should the first point be fifteen and the second thirty, while the third is only forty? The reasoning seems to be derived from French currency of the Middle Ages, which in turn derived from the ancient Babylonian obsession with the mystical significance of the number sixty. The 60 sous coin was the unit most commonly used for gambling in those days, so we are told, and the winner of the game would win the coin. There being four points to be won in each game, the players would shout that they had won 15, then 30 then 45 sous, before taking the game and the coin. The forty-five was shortened to forty because it was easier to say, and thus the scoring system was born. It's as likely as any other explanation, anyway. And "love" refers to the shape of the figure nought – the egg or, in French, *l'oeuf*.

The first Wimbledon championships attracted twenty-two entrants. The first match was between a Mr H.T. Gillson and Mr Spencer Gore, which Spencer Gore won. Gore, a local surveyor and an Old Harrovian who was then twenty-seven years old, went on to win the title, beating William Marshall in the final. The finals were not the major sporting occasion they have become, although the first prize, a "Silver Challenge Cup, value twenty-five guineas" was a valuable trophy which unquestionably compromised the players' amateur ideals. It was also worth more than the combined total of money received from the entrants' fees, one guinea each – total twenty-two guineas. The balance was made up by gate money from the spectators, who paid one shilling each.

The final was played on Thursday 19 July, because the original date set aside for the final, Monday 16 July, was wet. Although the semi-finals had been completed the previous Thursday (with Marshall gaining a bye to the final because the previous rounds had resulted in there being only three players left at the semi-final stage), the final was deliberately delayed beyond the weekend because it would otherwise have clashed with the Eton v Harrow cricket match at Lord's; and this match was undoubtedly the social event of the sporting season. Gore himself had played for Harrow for three years in a row from 1867, so no doubt was very keen to attend. Wisden describes the match in glowing terms:

"As fashionable as ever, the Eton v Harrow match of 1877 attracted to Lord's Ground, on the 13th of last July, one of those wondrous assemblages of rank and fashion of the country that previous gatherings may possibly have eclipsed in numbers but certainly not in influence or brilliancy."[3]

In fact, there were over 13,000 people there over the two days, 8,089 on the Friday and 5,327 on the Saturday, when it rained. This was indeed a total eclipsed in numbers by previous years. In 1873, for example, when Wimbledon's 1878 champion played for Harrow and played "one of the best innings seen in public-school cricket for many years",[4] 15,868 attended on the

Friday and 11,214 on the Saturday. But as the sycophantic Wisden reporter added:

"Aristocratic picnic parties on tops of drags, in old-fashion carriages, new-fashion wagonettes and various other vehicles proved the old match as irresistible as heretofore with that large section of fashionable London society who think the season incomplete unless they go to 'Harrow and Eton at Lord's'".

The Wimbledon final, when it was eventually played, attracted about two hundred spectators, little more than one per cent of the numbers who flocked to Lord's. A hundred and thirty years on, the roles are entirely reversed.

Spencer Gore was a volleyer, and in the final against the real-tennis player William Marshall, who played from the baseline, he won 6–1, 6–2, 6–4. There was much controversy at the time over the fairness of such tactics (along with equal debate about the merits of the overhead serve, first introduced by A.T. Myers in 1878), but Gore's style, being successful, was to prove long-lasting; or at least, although the volley was enthusiastically espoused by all future lawn-tennis players as an essential part of their armoury of shots, Gore's habit of volleying the ball before it had even crossed the net was outlawed in 1879, after a heated debate in the course of the final match of the 1878 tournament, which Gore eventually lost.

Gore never thought much of his own efforts, nor indeed of the sport in which he became the first champion. In 1892 he prophesied "that anyone who has played really well at cricket, tennis or even rackets, will ever seriously give his attention to lawn tennis...is extremely doubtful." He thought that the game was so monotonous that nobody would want to spend enough time practising to become expert. He proved a better tennis player than a prophet.

THE ANCIENT GAME OF TENNIS

The second Wimbledon championships were once again interrupted by the Eton v Harrow match (attendance 12,769), but once again, the champion was an Old Harrovian. This time it was a twenty-three-year-old tea planter called Patrick Francis Hadow, who was home on leave after three years in Ceylon and was persuaded by his elder brother Alexander to join him in taking part in the All England Lawn Tennis Championships while he was home. Though Alex Hadow was put out by Myers, the man with the overarm serve, Frank went on to win the challenge round against Spencer Gore, despite having sunstroke over the weekend of the Eton v Harrow match, and having to spend three days in bed. By the Wednesday following, Hadow merely had a splitting headache, but by using the lob against Gore, he won in three sets and introduced another new tactic to the fledgling world of lawn tennis. Several hundred people paid their shilling to watch the game. The tournament version of Wingfield's garden game was growing as rapidly in popularity as sphairistike had done a handful of summers before. Frank Hadow went back to Ceylon and never played serious tennis again (although the manner of his entry into the Wimbledon championships could hardly be called serious). He died in 1946, aged ninety-one, and goes down in history as the only champion ever to win every round in straight sets: the only man who has never lost a set at Wimbledon.

The early champions were a bizarre bunch. In 1879, because Frank Hadow was not defending his title, there was no challenge round, the winner of the main tournament being declared champion. This sad state of affairs, depriving the All England Club of the gate money for the challenge round, prompted Alex Hadow to write a letter to *The Times,* apologising for his brother's absence in Ceylon, but it also left the way

The Rev. John Thorneycroft Hartley winning the Lawn Tennis champion for
the second time in successive years against Herbert Fortescue Lawford in 1880

open for a new champion. It turned out to be John Hartley, a
man who had won a rackets Blue at Oxford in 1870 and was,
almost inevitably, another Old Harrovian. He was also clearly a
product of the vicarage tennis party form of the game, no doubt
at his own vicarage, because he was rector of Burneston,
between Thirsk and Northallerton in the North Riding of
Yorkshire. Wilfred Baddeley, writing in the *Windsor Magazine*
in 1895, the year he won his third Wimbledon singles title,
pointed out that "a noteworthy feature of lawn tennis is that the

professional element has never crept into it, as it has so largely into cricket, football and golf. No player who is not, in every sense of the word, an amateur, is allowed to take part in any tournament."[5] Hartley certainly lived up to this qualification, and when he reached the semi-final stage he must have been thankful for the three-day hiatus caused by the Eton v Harrow match. He hopped on a train to Thirsk and was able to carry out his priestly duties at home before catching the early train back again on the Monday morning. He reached King's Cross at about two o'clock and had to rush across London for his match against one C.F. Parr. He made it in time, but he arrived on court exhausted and without having eaten all day. Not surprisingly, Parr took the first set 6–2. Then, true to what was fast becoming a Wimbledon tradition, it began to rain. Hartley had time during the break to have tea, and when they got back on court he won the next three sets 6–0, 6–1, 6–1. He was in the final.

The final was certainly a case of good defeating evil. Eleven hundred people, the largest crowd yet, watched the Reverend John Hartley overcoming his opponent, who had been champion of Ireland but nevertheless insisted on playing under the pseudonym "St Leger", in three straight sets. The loser's real name was Goold, or Vere Thomas St Leger Goold to give him his full name. Hartley described him at the time as "a cheery wild Irishman" but in later years the wildness obviously overcame the cheeriness in his soul. In 1907, when he was fifty-three years old, he and his French wife Violet were arrested at Nice railway station when it was discovered that the contents of two trunks they were hoping to send to England were the remains of Mrs Emma Levin, a Danish widow with whom Mrs Goold evidently suspected her husband of having an affair. Goold tried to take all the blame on himself and was duly sentenced to life imprisonment. Even so, the judge did not believe that Goold's wife was an innocent party and sentenced her to death for the crime. Although Violet Goold was not in the end executed, St Leger Goold became the first, and so far only, Wimbledon finalist to be sent to the penal colony on Devil's Island off the coast of South America. He died there two years later, in 1909.

Tennis was now gaining a momentum of its own. Major Wingfield, Major Gem and J.H. Hale had all taken a back seat; the rules and the scoring system had been settled to the satisfaction of all; and championships were taking place in America, in France and in Ireland, as well as in several different parts of Britain. Needless to say, one of the early championship locations in England was Blackheath. This suburb of London has played a central role in the development of golf, soccer, rugby and hockey and obviously felt no wish to be left out of the growth of lawn tennis. But what tennis really needed was a true champion, a man to match on the tennis courts the deeds of W.G. Grace on the cricket field, and in 1881, it got one. Actually it got two – the Renshaw twins, William and Ernest, revolutionised lawn tennis.

The Renshaws were born on 3 January 1861 in Leamington, the birthplace of lawn tennis, or at least of Major Gem's version of it. They were just eighteen when they both first entered at Wimbledon, but in that first year neither of them actually played, both giving their opponents a walk-over. The next year, 1880, they came back, and this time they played, but both lost to the same man in successive rounds. Their conqueror, O.E. Woodhouse, who himself lost in the All Comers' final, did not know what an achievement his double success had been. He was the last person to beat William Renshaw in the

Ernest Renshaw, along with his older twin William, laid the foundations
of modern lawn tennis.

singles at Wimbledon until 1888, and usually it was only William who could beat his brother Ernest. As a doubles pair they were unrivalled. Their tactic of defeating the lob by taking the ball early with the "Renshaw Smash" was as revolutionary as Gore's use of the volley or John Hartley's original use of the lob. William Renshaw went on to be known as "the father of lawn tennis", a title that might have been awarded to Major Wingfield if only he had been able to play his own invention rather better than he did. When William beat the Reverend Mr Hartley in the challenge final of 1881 to take the title, he did so by the lopsided score of 6–0, 6–1, 6–1, a margin of victory that was not matched until 1936, when Fred Perry beat the German Gottfried von Cramm 6–1, 6–1, 6–0. The British have not won the Wimbledon men's singles title often, but when it happens, it is very one-sided.

The other great hero of the sport was Charlotte "Lottie" Dod. Dod won the Wimbledon ladies' singles at the age of fifteen in 1887, and is still the youngest Grand Slam champion of all time, even though she competed years before the idea of a Grand Slam existed. Wimbledon introduced a ladies' tournament in 1884, a move that was seen as remarkably daring in late Victorian times when it was still unseemly for a young woman to be seen to indulge in anything too strenuous or too competitive. But the Married Women's Property Act of 1882 had been a powerful symbol of the improving status of women in Victorian times, and the ladies' championships at Wimbledon were just another symptom of the changing times. The first winner was Maud Watson, who beat her elder sister Lilian in three sets to win the first prize, a "silver flower-basket, value twenty guineas". In view of Wilfred Baddeley's firm stance against professionalism, it is worth noting that Maud Watson's first prize in 1884 was of greater value than the first prize awarded to the great Maria Bueno when she beat the South African Sandra Reynolds three-quarters of a century later. Her prize in 1960 was a voucher worth just fifteen pounds.

These days great significance is put on the early participation of women in lawn tennis at the highest level, and certainly tennis was lucky at the beginning of its life to have two such great and charismatic ladies' champions as Maud Watson and Lottie Dod. Between them, they made the first moves to open the door for women to take part in all sporting competitions, almost forty years before women got the vote. But at the time there was no particular debate about introducing a ladies' championship. Women had taken part in lawn tennis from the beginning; much of its popularity at a social level was in its role in the complicated courtship rituals of the shy middle classes, making it genuinely a game in which the two sexes could mix to the full. There were no concessions to the needs of the sport when it came to the clothes the ladies wore. With long sleeves, full-length skirts, petticoats, corsets and bustles, it was a wonder they could even move around the court, let alone hit the ball with pace and accuracy. It must have been difficult to play wearing a tennis apron over the skirts (complete with large pockets to put the balls in), tight high-buttoned blouses and straw boaters which were the uniform of the day, but Lottie Dod did it far better than anybody else.

Lottie Dod was a prodigy at all sports, and a child prodigy at tennis. She was born on 24 September 1871 and won her first important title in 1882 – the ladies' doubles at the Northern Tournament in Manchester – at the age of eleven. Her partner was her nineteen-year-old sister Ann. By the age of twelve, she was beating many men, partly perhaps because she

Charlotte 'Lottie' Dod, five times winner of Wimbledon, won her first championship at the age of 15 and was never once beaten there

was too young to be distracted by their maleness, but mainly because she had learned the lessons of volleying and smashing taught by Spencer Gore and the Renshaws. She was never defeated at the Wimbledon championships, and only ever lost five singles matches in her entire career. That she won only five years out of seven from 1887 is because she did not compete in 1889 and 1890, as she found it all too easy. In 1889, after winning two finals in consecutive years against Blanche Hillyard (née Bingley), she took a summer holiday during the Wimbledon week and went boating with her sister off the west coast of Scotland instead. In 1891, 1892 and 1893 she came back to Wimbledon, and beat Blanche Hillyard in the final every year. Eventually she lost interest in lawn tennis altogether and turned her hand to golf, hockey and archery. In 1898 and 1899 she was a semi-finalist in the British ladies' golf championship, while in 1899 and 1900 she played hockey for England. In 1904 she won the ladies' golf title, beating May Hezlet by one hole in the final at Troon, and in 1905 as defending champion she arranged an impromptu international match just before the championships with the American sisters Harriot and Margaret Curtis. This was the seed that led, much later, to the establishment of the Curtis Cup competition between the amateur lady golfers of Britain and America. To round off her sporting career, in 1908 she won a silver medal at archery in the Olympic Games, held that year in London.

The one person who rejoiced in Miss Dod's retirement from tennis was Blanche Hillyard. Mrs Hillyard first competed at Wimbledon, as Miss Bingley, in the first ladies' competition in 1884, when she was nineteen years old. She was beaten by the eventual winner, Maud Watson, in the semi-final, but went on to reach the final in nine of the next ten years, and thirteen

All-comers' match at Wimbledon, 5th round, 1881.
Lawford v Renshaw

times in all. She married Commander George Hillyard in 1887, and made her last appearance at Wimbledon in 1913, when she was forty-nine years old. She won the title six times, the first in 1886 and the last in 1900, seven years before her husband was appointed secretary of the All England Club, a post he held until he retired in 1924. Tennis was always a family sport, and the Hillyards were just one more family in the line that began with the Renshaw twins, the Dod sisters, the Watson sisters and the Doherty brothers, Reggie (Big Do) and Laurie (Little Do), who dominated tennis at the turn of the century. It stretches past the Sterrys, mother Charlotte who won Wimbledon five times and daughter Gwen who played in the Wightman Cup; the Truman sisters; Vera Sukova, her son Cyril and her daughter Helena; and the McEnroe brothers, all the way to the Williams sisters of today.

By the end of the century, tennis was established as a leading sport, for playing and watching all around the world. It was so popular that it was chosen as one of the original sports included in the first modern Olympic Games in 1896. The medal in the men's singles was won by the otherwise undistinguished J.P. Boland of Britain, who also won the doubles playing with a German, Herr F. Traun. It was said that one of the competitors in the singles entered simply because it was the only way he could book a tennis court to play in Athens that day. He was an Englishman, of course.

Tennis developed all the time further and further away from the idea that Major Wingfield had patented. New strokes were employed, such as Gore's volley, Hadow's lob and the Renshaw smash, and new tactics were worked out to counter them. Perhaps the most influential of all players in the first fifty years of the sport's history was an American, Maurice McLoughlin. Born in 1890 in Carson City, Nevada, McLoughlin was brought up in San Francisco, where he played mainly on asphalt surfaces rather than grass. He won the Pacific States championship in 1907, and became national champion in 1912 and 1913. He was known as the "California Comet", which gives away his secret: he was the first top-class player to rely on a serve and volley game. The speed of his cannonball serve was something that many players found hard to cope with, and even though the Great War meant that he had only a short time at the very top, his style of play changed the whole pattern of men's tennis for ever. What is more, because Maurice

McLoughlin was the first champion to make it from the courts in the public parks, and not from the élite tennis clubs which had spawned all earlier champions, he did a great deal to spread the popularity of the game through all levels in the United States. He was a long way, in both style and geography, from Walter Wingfield's Christmas party at Nantclwyd.

Walter Clopton Wingfield died at the age of seventy-eight in 1912, the year that McLoughlin first won the US title. He is still remembered as the inventor of tennis, indeed he was described in a recent survey as one of the most influential inventors of all time. He himself had long since moved on from his sphairistike to other things; one of his later books was entitled *Bicycle Gymkhana*.

"ANCIENT AND HEALTHFUL EXERCISE OF THE GOLF"

Golf, the national game of Scotland, is the oldest of all ball games still played today. It is also one of the few ball games, like croquet and snooker but almost no others, in which the ball is motionless when it is played. It is certainly the only ball game in which each player plays with a different ball and makes no attempt to obstruct his opponent's play. Golf is a game where the opponent is not the person hacking round with you: the opponent is yourself. The course occasionally appears to be the opponent, but it is, in reality, impartial and refuses to take sides, despite extreme provocation now and again.

The true origins of golf are as vague as the origins of practically all ball games. The game was possibly invented by the Dutch, a theory that devolves from paintings of men in Holland in the 16th century playing a game that looks like a cross between golf and ice hockey, called "kolf". Kolf was played on frozen canals with a club and a small wooden ball. The Dutch were a busy maritime trading race, and we know that they bought wool from Scotland where the coastal areas were home to vast flocks of sheep, so it is easy to believe that kolf travelled with them, and found a happy home on the eastern seaboard of Scotland. But then there is the mediaeval

A print of an early form of golf from the pages of *Every Boy's* annual

French game, *jeu de mail*, which is played by hitting a ball across vast distances, the Belgian game of "chole", with a similar theme, and even the ancient Roman game of "paganica", which involved using a bent wooden stick to hit balls made of leather and stuffed with feathers. Golf's family tree has deep roots and its branches spread in many different directions.

As we have already seen, golf enjoyed royal patronage in Scotland from its earliest beginnings there. Mary Queen of Scots was much criticised for being seen out on the links enjoying herself only a few days after the mysterious death of her husband Lord Darnley in 1567. Her son, James VI of Scotland and James I of England, was a very enthusiastic golfer, even though he had very nearly been assassinated by a conspiracy of golfing men. On 5 August 1600, three years before he became King of England and was making do with the kingdom of

Scotland, James was lured to Gowrie Castle near Perth and taken into a room in one of the castle's highest towers where, legend would have us believe, an armed and fully prepaid assassin was waiting to kill him. The main villains of the piece were Alexander Ruthven and his brother John, Earl of Gowrie, and the story goes that Ruthven held a dagger to the king's heart and threatened to kill him, but somehow James managed to talk himself out of the dire situation and with the help of his own men, defeated the assassination attempt. Ruthven and Gowrie were killed in the fracas which followed, but the subsequent investigation into the plot cast suspicion on the Logan family of Restalrig as co-conspirators. The Privy Council of Scotland duly summoned Halbert Logan to account for his actions, and sent an officer to fetch him. Halbert was found on the golf course at Lochend, near Edinburgh, so absorbed in his game that he refused to break off for such an unimportant engagement as pleading for his life before the Privy Council. He used what Robert Clark, an early writer on the game, described as "despiteful language" to the man who had come to arrest him, and carried on playing. A warrant was duly issued for his arrest, so Logan "mounted a fleet horse, and fled to England".[1] His tactic for avoiding arrest worked, and in the process he proved that golf is life, and stopping playing is the same as death.

Once King James moved south and added England to his collection of kingdoms, he began playing regularly at Blackheath, a course which he had marked out himself so that he could indulge his passion for golf without having to make the long march to Scotland every time he felt like a round. Despite his royal station, or perhaps because of it, James was also aware of the commercial possibilities of the game. In 1603, he appointed William Mayne, a bowmaker living in Edinburgh, as clubmaker to the king for life, and over the next few years he became increasingly alarmed at the number of golf balls that were being brought into his realm from overseas, and the massive negative balance of trade that this represented. We do not know where these balls were being made, although the two most obvious suspects are France, where Mary Queen of Scots had spent much of her life in exile and where we know she played golf often, and Holland, where they played kolf on ice. A decree of 1618 noted that "no small quantity of gold and silver is transported yearly out of his highness's kingdom of Scotland for buying golf balls" so King James promptly banned their importation and appointed James Melvill the sole manufacturer of golf balls in the kingdom for a period of twenty-one years, providing that he did not charge more than four shillings per ball – an enormous price compared with today. It seems obvious from the fact that Melvill was appointed for a limited time and that he was given an upper limit on the price he could charge, that Mr Mayne the clubmaker with a lifetime's right to make clubs for the king was charging outrageous prices and eliminating competition by means of his royal decree. The first golf millionaires were being created, and as always, it was the makers of the weaponry rather than the users who were making the killing.

The balls which Melvill made were simple enough to play with, but quite difficult to manufacture. These were the days of the "featherie" ball, which took over from a little wooden pellet, probably in the 15th century, as the game of golf developed separately from the games of pall mall and croquet, to which it was once closely related. Pall mall was a kind of target golf, requiring a straight-walled alley up to half a mile long, which gave its name to the street in London where King James VI and

I played the game when he was not playing golf. It was played with a hard ball and a stick which resembled a croquet mallet more than a golf club.

The feather golf ball consisted of a leather casing, usually made of two or three sections stitched together, which was stuffed with boiled goose feathers. We do not know who had the great idea of stuffing boiled goose feathers into a little leather case to make a golf ball. It is such a bizarre stuffing material that we are forced to wonder what options were rejected before boiled goose feathers were decreed to be the perfect material. Once the feathers had been stuffed into the little leather globe, the outer case was stitched up and painted white, thus creating an airtight seal. Inside the casing, the goose feathers would expand and the pressure they exerted on the leather casing made the ball bounce in a lively manner.

Clearly, the amount of goose feathers that were stuffed into the casing would prove crucial to the bounciness of the ball, and ball makers who could get it right more often than not were highly prized. James Melvill, of course, had the entire market to himself until 1639 which gave him a head start in the technology. The bounciness of his products was attested to by the tragic case of one Thomas Chatto, who was killed in 1632 in Kelso churchyard when he was hit by one of Melvill's more deadly missiles. Poor Thomas had apparently been "lurking in the churchyard while golf was in progress", a nice twist on the more common 20th century grumble about people lurking on the golf course while church is in progress. As if to prove that going to church is a far more dangerous pastime than playing golf, Chatto was hit under his left lung by a well-struck if poorly directed shot by an unnamed golfer, and perished forthwith. At least it would not have cost much to transport him to his place of burial. If the sermon at his funeral was performed by the minister of St Andrews at about that time, Robert Blair, poor Thomas would have had scant comfort as he made his way towards the pearly gates. Blair regularly used golfing metaphors in his sermons, including his often repeated opinion that God was joined to his church as closely as the head of a golf club was to its shaft. This was perhaps a two-edged compliment, because even in those days there were plenty of instances of the clubhead breaking loose during the course of a round. William Mayne's artefacts were no more perfect than the people who used them.

Melvill's monopoly was only maintained by employing many other golf ball makers to work as sub-contractors for him, and after the death of King James in 1625 many people felt that Melvill's rights had died with his sovereign. In 1629, the brothers Thomas and William Dickson of Leith accused Melvill of using violent methods to enforce the monopoly, or in their words "exacting a certain impost aff everie gowffe ball made within this kingdome". According to the Dicksons, Melvill had ordered soldiers to confiscate nineteen golf balls from the Dickson workshop. As each ball took several hours to make, this confiscation represented perhaps a week's production, and a potential turnover of nearly ten pounds, so it was not surprising that the Dicksons were upset. The Scottish law lords of the Edinburgh Privy Council decided that Melvill had lost his monopoly on the death of the king (a decision that did not, apparently, set a precedent across the entire British Isles: Melvill went on exacting his dues elsewhere) and fined him for his brutality. Making golf balls in those days was no fun, so the Dicksons deserved any money and sympathy that their industry could provide them. The work of stuffing the leather balls was hard and difficult, and the lead paints and boiled goose-feather dust led to chronic chest problems which not even a bracing round of golf over the best Scottish links could dispel.

In the 1640s, after Melvill had finally lost his monopoly on golf ball supply, we learn of the Marquess of Montrose playing regularly at St Andrews and at Leith (home of the Dicksons), where he bought two golf balls for ten shillings, an increase of a shilling a ball over the price that King James I had fixed in 1618. There was another Dickson, John of that ilk, who in 1642 was appointed by Aberdeen town council to make and sell featheries in the area of their jurisdiction, but we do not know if he was a relation. We do know that his prices were no cheaper. Clearly, when you sliced a ball into the wide blue yonder, or into the rib cage of a passing Scotsman, in the 17th century, you spent a great deal of time making sure you got the ball back, or else you would be severely out of pocket.

King James VII and II, grandson of James VI and I, was another keen golfer, if less scrupulous in his methods. In 1681, when he was still Duke of York and therefore confusingly living in Edinburgh, he got into a discussion with two English nobles about which country had the better golfers. Some sources suggest that it was not a discussion, it was an argument, and it was about the fundamental issue of where golf had originated. This seems highly unlikely. There is some small case for arguing that golf may have started on continental Europe and grown up in Scotland, but there is no possibility that it began in England. The English noblemen were either very stupid (always a possibility) or very tactless to argue against their future king on these grounds, but there would have been more substance to an argument about which country had the better golfers in 1681.

So the first-ever international golf match was organised, although the Duke of York, with an English title, was qualified for both countries. It was decided that the game would take place around the Leith links, and the teams would be the two English nobles against James, Duke of York and any Scotsman of his choice. The Duke already had a Scottish golfing companion, yet another Dickson from Leith, first name Andrew, who was his forecaddie; it was his job to carry the royal clubs and show where the royal ball had landed. The Duke sought Dickson's advice and chose John Patersone, a shoemaker who was also well known as one of the best players of his day. Being a shoemaker and thus having plenty of offcuts of leather, it is entirely possible that Patersone augmented his business by making golf balls as well, which would have given the Scottish pair a further advantage. The stake for the match was high, not only in terms of national honour but also in terms of the money.

It proved to be all very one-sided. The Duke and Patersone won, easily beating the English lords. The Duke split the stake with Patersone – perhaps fifty fifty, perhaps not – and although we do not know the amount of the wager, Patersone's share was enough to build himself a house in Edinburgh, in Canongate. He called the house "The Golfer's Land", and it stood for two hundred years and more. He had a coat of arms built into the wall, surmounted by a crest of a hand clutching a golf club, with the motto "Far and Sure", which was later adopted by the Royal and Ancient Golf Club at St Andrews who still use it today. The wall also bore an additional inscription, "I Hate No Person", which is an anagram of "John Patersone" (substituting the J for an I). It is not known whether no person hated John Patersone in return. The two English lords would have been expected to bear at least a slight grudge, but etiquette, that aspect of a golfer's skills which is these days found in no other sport, would have prevented them from showing it.

Gambling was the main interest in the sport at this time, just as it was with every other sport that attracted public interest. John Patersone was certainly not the only man before the 20th-century to have made a fortune from his golfing skills. In 1724, Alexander Elphinstone (whose elder brother Arthur would die on the scaffold twenty-two years later) challenged Captain John Porteous of the Edinburgh City Guard (who himself would be hanged by a vengeful mob in Edinburgh on 7 September 1736) to "a solemn match at golf" for a stake of twenty guineas. This was such a large sum that it attracted a vast crowd to watch the game, including the Duke of Hamilton and the Earl of Morton (whose ancestor had employed James Melvill as his quartermaster), and "a vast mob of great and little besides". Elphinstone won.

The stake may have been deemed large by Edinburgh's golfing fraternity, but in comparison with the sums being wagered on horses, cricket and prize fighting in London at the time, it was small beer and of course not in any way attributable to the supposed tightfistedness of the Scots people. In Scotland, golf had always been the people's game, a game for the poor as well as for the rich, and despite the best attempts of the Anglicised nobility to change things, it has always remained so. The first golf club to be formed was the Edinburgh Burgess Club, in 1735, followed shortly by the Gentlemen Golfers of Edinburgh, a group which was later to become the Honourable Company of Edinburgh Golfers. This does not suggest that the Edinburgh gentlemen were originally dishonourable, but they were certainly just a cross-section of Edinburgh middle classes rather than a group of people who prided themselves on their breeding. On 7 March 1744, the "gentlemen of honour skilful in the ancient and healthful exercise of the golf" asked

A pen-drawing from 1863 by C.A. Doyle showing gentleman golfers at play

Edinburgh City Council to present them with a silver golf club to be presented to the winner of their annual competition over Leith links, a request which was duly granted. We are forced to the conclusion that several of the leaders of Edinburgh City Council were also members of the Gentlemen Golfers, but their main achievement was not in presenting a remarkable prize. The significance of this barely selfless action was that a set of rules had for the first time to be written down, so that all those competing for the prize would know that the competition had been fair.

The minutes of the Edinburgh Council state clearly that "the Gentlemen Golfers had drawn up a scroll at the desire of the Magistrates, of such articles and conditions...to be observed by the Gentlemen who should yearly offer to play for the said Silver Club". So it was the magistrates who insisted that golf should have rules, no doubt hoping that the process of drawing them up would provide plenty of work for the legal profession. In this they were no doubt disappointed because they managed in just thirteen articles to encapsulate the essence of the game to the satisfaction of all. It is a remarkable coincidence that the earliest extant rules of both golf and cricket should date from the same year. 1744 was an important one in the growth of sporting pursuits in Britain.

All the main customs and regulations of modern golf are here: "you are not to change the ball which you strike off the tee", "you are not to remove stones, bones or any break club for the sake of playing your ball, except on the fair green" – a reminder that bones, from dead livestock, were a major hazard two hundred and fifty years ago. There is another article governing balls striking "any person, horse, dog or anything else". The anything else in question might in those days have included all kinds of distractions, ranging from games of football to flocks of sheep, huntsmen complete with horses and hounds, or women hanging out the family washing.

"If your ball comes among watter, or any wattery filth, you are at liberty to take out your ball and bringing it behind the hazard and teeing it, you may play it with any club and allow your adversary a stroke for so getting out your ball." Those of us who have fished their balls out of "wattery filth" plenty of times will recognise this article at once.

There were other articles covering lost balls, touching balls, broken clubs and the rule of golf etiquette that "he whose ball lyes farthest from the hole is obliged to play first". What was not specified is how many holes there should be, or whether there should be a standard length for courses. At the Leith links in those days there were just five holes, each of over four hundred yards in length, a major undertaking for golfers armed with only wooden clubs and featherie balls, and wearing clothes not designed to make swinging a golf club any easier. St Andrews had twenty-two holes, while Blackheath in England had started out as a seven-hole course. At St Andrews, players originally played eleven holes one way, and then came back through the same eleven in reverse. As the game became more popular, it became difficult to have two different sets of golfers trying to play the same hole at different times in their rounds, so the fairways were widened, with just the greens being used twice. Then in 1764, William St Clair of Roslin shot the unimaginably low score of 121 for the twenty-two holes, and in response to this feat, the St Andrews committee reduced the first four holes to two, which had the effect of lengthening the course to prevent such low scores being achieved again. It also meant that there were now nine holes each way, eighteen in all. This eventually became the standard for all courses. William St Clair, incidentally, was also the Grand Master of the Masons of Scotland in his day, showing that under the English influence, golf was becoming as élitist a game north of the border as it was already in the south.

The winner of the first Silver Club competition at Leith was John Rattray, a surgeon from Edinburgh who was also the leading light in drawing up the thirteen articles. He won it again the next year, but on 22 September 1745 he was called away to Prestonpans, nine miles away, to tend to the wounded after the battle there between the English Royalists, led by Sir John Cope, and the Jacobites, under Prince Charles Edward,

William St Clair of Roslin as captain of the Hon. company of
Edinburgh golfers

which ended in a rare victory for the home side. Rattray cared for the Jacobite wounded, and then was persuaded to accompany the rebels south as they chased the remnants of Cope's army towards the border and beyond. He stayed with the army as their fortunes changed and they retreated north again, and was captured at Culloden.

He was saved from execution at the hands of the Duke of Cumberland (who, as we know, was more interested in gambling his fortune on prize fighting than playing golf) by the intervention of a fellow member of the Gentlemen Golfers, Duncan Forbes, who was Lord President of the Court of Sessions. On this occasion, the unhappy knack that great golfers seem to have had of joining a losing cause had a happy ending. Arthur Elphinstone, another Culloden prisoner of war and the elder brother of Alexander who had beaten Porteous in 1724, was obviously not so well connected; nor were his head and shoulders after his date with the executioner on Tower Hill. Posterity owes a great deal to John Rattray, but he scooped most of what he was owed during his lifetime by drafting the rules for a major sporting competition which he himself could win. This example was followed by Charles Alcock in football a hundred and twenty years later.

Golf was already spreading its wings overseas by this time. As long ago as 1650, a man called Jacob Jansz was arrested in Albany, New Amsterdam (to become New York fourteen years later) for using a golf club to attack a fellow drinker in a local tavern. In 1734, golf clubs were being exported from Scotland to Carolina, but the game failed to take general hold in the Americas for another century and a half, despite the formation of the South Carolina Golf Club in 1786, ten years after the declaration of American independence.

It was in 1834 during the reign of Queen Victoria's uncle, the "Sailor King" William IV, five years after the formation of India's first golf club in Calcutta, that the St Andrews Golf Club received the title of "Royal and Ancient". The club had been formed in 1754, eight years after Culloden, by "twenty-two Noblemen and Gentlemen being admirers of the ancient and healthful exercise of golf", and quickly established itself as a social and sporting rival to the Edinburgh Company. This description of golf as an "ancient and healthful exercise" echoes exactly the words used by the Gentlemen Golfers when they petitioned Edinburgh Council for their Silver Club trophy, so either the same man wrote the two documents or else it was the way the game was always described. St Andrews was the second club on which William bestowed the title "Royal", after the Perth Golf Society, which received the Royal prefix in 1833. King William realised the pre-eminence of St Andrews, though, as he also presented the King William IV Gold Medal to them in the last year of his life, 1837. The inscription read that it was presented by the King to "the Royal and Ancient Golph Club of St Andrews", a variation in the spelling of the game that is a sign of His Majesty's idiosyncratic nature or else his dyslexia. His widow, Queen Adelaide, who we have already come across standing on the touchline at Rugby School cheering on the boys and among whose many titles was that of Duchess of St Andrews, presented the Royal Adelaide Medal to the club in 1838, showing her all-round interest in sports.

The earliest surviving golf clubs are on display at the Royal Troon Golf Club. There are eight of them, six wooden clubs and two irons, which were found in a bricked up cupboard in Hull, of all places, together with a newspaper dated 1741. The paper is a clue, if not necessarily a reliable one, to their age, but we can safely assume that they date from the first quarter of the 18th century. The wooden clubs of this period were made with ash shafts and long heads of thorn, apple, pear or beech. The irons were rarely used because they tended to rip into the featherie balls, which, as we have seen, were very expensive. Most players would prefer to drop a stroke or two than have to buy a new ball. The irons were simply to get out of trouble, with contemporary records talking of "bonker clubbis" which we can assume to mean clubs for use in bunkers, rather than clubs with which to hit one's opponent or passing rabbits, or indeed clubs to be used in some kind of modern sexual act. (The use of the word "bonk" in what has become its present slang meaning is also sports connected: the first recorded usage was in *Foul* magazine, the first football fanzine, in 1974.) Your average Sunday morning medal golfer, or his 18th century equivalent, would have taken probably four clubs out on the course with him, three woods and one iron, which were enough to cope with the vagaries of the open links of those days, and to minimise the risk of losing a precious featherie. This is ten fewer than the number allowed these days.

After William Mayne, we do not know the names of the great club-makers until James McEwan, who began marking his clubs with his name in 1770. Others followed his example, like Simon Cossar of Leith, Henry Miln at St Andrews, John Jackson of Perth and Thomas Comb of Bruntsfield. Some of these men were golf professionals, whose main business was in keeping the courses in good condition or teaching their club members how to play, and they had little understanding of how to make a golf club. So they merely sold their names and some technical advice, like Walter Hagen, Arnold Palmer and a hundred others were to do in years to come, to be put on the clubs by the maker. The people who actually made the clubs were the experts – carpenters or furniture-makers who could recognise a profitable sideline when they saw one. Perhaps the best of these was Hugh Philp, a local St Andrews joiner who repaired golf clubs in his spare time. By 1819, his reputation was such that he was appointed official club-maker to what was in those pre-King William IV days the Society of St Andrews Golfers. He was a stern-looking man, with a brusque way with people, but such was his skill as a club-maker that other makers forged his mark on their inferior clubs in order to pump up the price for which they could sell them – the first known instance of a sports equipment brand being greater than the product.

Philp died in 1856, having taken on his nephew Robert Forgan in 1852 to carry on his business. Forgan proved to be as brilliant a club-maker as businessman, and he expanded the company he inherited into one of the biggest sports businesses of its time. But before Philp died, the biggest change in the way golf is played had taken place, and without that change, the game and the industry that it supports could not have grown as fast as it did. From 1848, the featherie gave way to the "guttie".

Despite royal patronage, or perhaps because of it, golf in the early 19th century was becoming a more and more élite pastime, even in Scotland. The cost of clubs and balls was prohibitive for all but the most well-off, and the social times did not favour public extravagance. Whereas a hundred and fifty years later farmers were selling their land to golf-course developers, in the 1820s it was the other way around, with immense pressure being put on golf clubs to free up some or all of their land for agricultural purposes. In the 1840s, there were just a handful of golf clubs left in all of Scotland and very few in England, and those that survived did so with few players. Support for this élite and personal game was being swept away by the social and economic pressures of the times. Just when all seemed lost, salvation appeared in the unlikely form of a parcel from Asia.

In 1845, Dr Robert Patterson, a priest based in St Andrews, was the man who received this revolutionary package. It contained a statue of Vishnu, the Hindu god of preservation, from a friend in East Asia. However interesting the statue itself might have been, the reverend doctor was even more interested in the packing material, an off-white springy substance which kept Vishnu in a state of fine preservation throughout its journey. The substance was gutta-percha, a latex derivative which had every quality that a golfer could desire to make the perfect ball. And Dr Patterson, like most of his congregation, was a golfer. Gutta-percha was springy and malleable when hot but hard and bouncy when cold. It was far easier to mould into the shape of a golf ball than the laborious featheries, and Dr Patterson saw its potential immediately. Within a couple of years, his patented balls were being used everywhere, having first been tried in England where the power of the traditional club- and ball-makers was less obvious. The advantage of the new gutties over the old featheries was not only in the aerodynamics – they flew much farther – but also in cost. A guttie could be sold profitably for a shilling (5p), compared with at least half a crown (12.5p) for each featherie. Douglas Gourlay, the leading maker of featherie balls (and at the top end of the market, selling his featheries for four to five shillings each), saw the writing on the wall very quickly. After taking part in a trial of the new gutties he decided to get rid of his complete stock of featheries by sending nine dozen to one of his regular customers, Sir David Baird of North Berwick, who was thus probably the last man in Britain still to be using the featheries. Nine dozen would have represented perhaps three weeks' production but at least three years' play, and they would have cost Sir David over twenty pounds. Gourlay was a canny businessman.

The man who was most affected by the demise of the featherie (apart from Dr Patterson, who no doubt made a few shillings from the success of his gutta-percha patent) was a man called Allan Robertson. In all the history of golf, it is doubtful that there has been a more influential figure. He was born in 1815, the son and grandson of golf professionals, and he became not only the greatest golfer of his age but also the most sought-after manufacturer of featherie balls. In 1844 he was reputed to have made 2,456 balls, an average of between six and seven balls a day throughout the year, a massive rate of production. If he sold them at two shillings and sixpence, he would have earned a gross amount of £307 in that year, to add to his earnings as a teacher and caddy to the members at St Andrews.

The guttie ball represented a huge challenge to his way of life, and for some time he persisted in believing that the featherie was better. It was, but only when he played with one, because he could have played with a football and still have beaten most men in Scotland, which in those days by definition meant the world. Featherie balls certainly became soggy and unplayable in the rain – a not uncommon meteorological phenomenon in Scotland – but the guttie balls also had problems at first. They tended to fly poorly even when hit well and often dipped suddenly in flight. It is said that when Allan Robertson was asked to try out one of the new gutties, he deliberately topped the ball and declared that they would never be any good, but lesser players quickly saw their merits. They were much cheaper and a sliced shot rarely sliced the ball in two. Such was the immediate success of the new ball that Robertson began paying local lads to go out on the course and find all the gutties they could, often even before they were lost, so that he could dispose of them in the fire that burned late into the night in his workshop.

Robertson's stubbornness meant that he fell out with his own leading apprentice, Tom Morris, whom he found playing with gutties on the Old Course. Morris was another brilliant golfer and also a fine maker of featherie balls for Robertson. It was his reputation as a golfer, though, that created enough interest in his golf balls for one of his featheries, made in 1845, to be sold at auction by Phillips in 1993 for £17,825, about ninety thousand times the original price. Tom Morris left Allan Robertson and St Andrews in 1851 and went to become keeper of the greens at Prestwick, at a salary of fifteen shillings a week. His disagreement with his old boss proved to be highly significant a few years later. Yet Robertson's defence of the featherie eventually proved untenable. By the mid-1850s, even the great Allan Robertson was persuaded of the merits of the guttie, and showing the strength of purpose that carried all before him on the golf course, he set about creating a factory for producing the best gutties in Britain, in the most efficient way. The fifty-year era of the guttie had begun.

Robertson's influence on golf was not limited to his golf-ball production skills, nor even to his skills as a player. He was also a great innovator in technique and in creating golf clubs to suit his particular style. It was Robertson who was the inspiration behind all sorts of new clubs with strange names like the baffie, the spoon, the cleek, the bulger and the mashie. He created clubs with heads of different sizes set at different angles, to take over from the less scientific "trouble" clubs, and he went round every golf course he played in fewer shots than any of his

Tom Morris Senior in 1880

rivals. He was said never to have lost a singles match playing on level terms (although his father must have beaten him a few times when he was still a lad), and is certainly the man first credited with going round the Old Course at St Andrews in less than 80.

Such was Robertson's skill on the golf course that his fame spread far beyond the links. People in Scotland wanted to find out if he really was as good as he was supposed to be, especially as many thought that Tom Morris was the better player. But since their argument in 1851, the two had never played against each other. Both had played against the other leading players of the age, like Willie Park, Andrew Strath and Willie Dunn, but the results were inconclusive when considering which of the two great players was the best. Robertson continued to refuse to play in any match, singles or doubles, with or against Tom Morris. So in 1855, the Prestwick club, Morris's employer, proposed a championship to decide the issue. To lure Robertson on to the starting tee, they proposed that the championship be held at St Andrews. However, the authorities at the Royal and Ancient took their time in replying, so much so that the Prestwick club gave up waiting and turned to Musselburgh to see if they would stage the championship. Musselburgh was the course where, on 14 December 1810, the first-ever golf competition for women had been staged – a tournament for the local fishwives. But Musselburgh did not respond quickly either, and by this time three full golfing seasons had passed. Then the saga took a tragic turn: Allan Robertson died suddenly from jaundice in 1859, so the issue could never be finally decided. The Prestwick club, however, decided that they wanted their man to be proclaimed champion of all Scotland so in 1860, they went ahead with a championship, and held it at their own course.

This was what is now recognised as the first Open Championship.

Archibald Montgomerie, the thirteenth Earl of Eglinton, was the driving force behind the championship. He was a hugely wealthy Tory politician as well as being the local laird, and he had an impressive track record of organising major sporting events. On 28 August 1839, he had held the Eglinton Tournament in the grounds of his castle, a revival of the mediaeval tournaments that had been Europe's first mass sporting events half a millennium earlier. The cost was reported to be between thirty and forty thousand pounds but as a contemporary report stated, "the week's pageant was entirely spoiled by rain". Fifteen knights, fully kitted out in suits of armour, "tilted in ancient fashion, breaking their spears in the jousts and finally paying their devoirs to the queen of beauty, Lady Seymour." The mud must have matched anything seen on a rugby pitch at around the same time.

Twenty-one years later, he brought his money and his organisational skills to what is now recognised as the first Open Championship. In those days Prestwick was a 3,799 yard twelve-hole course and it decided to make the championship a strokeplay competition over three rounds for professionals only, for a first prize of a belt valued at thirty guineas. It was given the exciting title of the "General Golf Tournament of Scotland". The lure of this title, the belt and the money attracted just eight men: Tom Morris of Prestwick, Willie Park, the Musselburgh champion, Bob Andrew (who rejoiced in the nickname of "The Rook"), Charles Hunter, Alexander Smith, William Steel, Andrew Strath and, at the last minute, George Daniel Brown, the professional of the Royal Blackheath Club on the Kentish edge of London. Brown's entry was at first questioned by the

Golfers at Blackheath, 1790

organising committee, who were not sure that a golf tournament of Scotland should include players from England, but as
Brown was actually an expatriate Scot, he was allowed in. There
may have been another reason for their reluctance: when the
Prestwick club had in 1857 run a tournament for pairs of
golfers, the Blackheath pair had won the competition, beating
the Royal and Ancient team in the final, and immediately

Blackheath started calling itself "The Champion Golf Club of the World". The tournament was not repeated (thus allowing Blackheath to retain their self-styled title indefinitely), but there is little doubt that the Prestwick club did not want another English victory. They wanted a native Scot to win, and more especially their man, Tom Morris.

Lord Eglinton's eye for detail stretched as far as the outfits that the professionals wore. At this time it was common for golfers to wear club jackets when playing, and for example there was a rule at the Blackheath club which stated that "members shall appear in their Red Coats on the Medal Days" but this dress code does not seem to have applied to the professionals, who were a scruffy lot, in stark contrast with the golfers of today. Scruffiness extended into indecent exposure in some cases, apparently, so loose fitting were some of the professionals' outfits. Furthermore, they liked a drink or two, and there are stories of Willie Park, among others, spending the night in gaol during and after the tournament, to sleep off his celebrations. The noble Lord Eglinton decided that it would not do for the sensitivities of the female members of the gallery to be affronted by the well-ventilated clothing of the players, so he gave each player a suit in the Eglinton tartan to wear on the course.

They played with guttie balls, of course, and Tom Morris, the local and the bookies' favourite, set the pace. He came in from the first round with a 58, but in the group behind, Willie Park, the white-bearded champion from Musselburgh, shot a 55. As the golfing correspondent of the *Ayr Advertiser* pointed out, Morris and his supporters were "buoying themselves on hope of him recovering himself in the second round". But he shot a 59 in the second round, a score which Park matched, so as they went into the final round, Park held a three-stroke lead.

Nobody else was in contention. Although Morris (58, 59, 59) caught up one shot on the final round, Park won by two shots with a total of 174 (55, 59, 60). He was presented with the belt, and it was immediately decided that the next year's championship would be "open to the world". The next year the world comprised twelve men, and the winner this time was Tom Morris. It was not until his son, Tom Morris Jr, won in 1868 that one of the original eight competitors in 1860 failed to take the belt.

Tom Morris Jr is still regarded as one of the greatest golfers of all time, and his skills resulted in two changes to the way the Open was run. Firstly, the organising committee decided that after eleven years it was time to move the championship to other courses. This may also have been partly due to the fact that Lord Eglinton had died in 1861, so his drive (and probably his money) was just a distant memory by 1871. Still, the move was overdue. In all the years the competition had been held at Prestwick, it never attracted more than the seventeen competitors who turned up in 1870, but as soon as it moved to other courses, the numbers leapt. The first Open held at St Andrews, in 1873, attracted twenty-six competitors, and the first at Musselburgh the next year brought thirty-two men to the starting tee. The first time the Open came south into England, to the Royal St George's at Sandwich in 1894, there were a record ninety-four entrants.

Secondly, by winning the belt outright in 1870 on his third consecutive victory, Morris forced the organising committee to think of another prize. They eventually came up with a little claret jug. This is still the prize today, and undoubtedly the most famous and most coveted trophy in golf. It actually took them over a year to create this trophy, with the result that the

Open was not held in 1871 because Young Tom had taken the belt home to keep and was not interested in letting anybody else play for a trophy he had won outright. When the Open was resumed in 1872, he became the first winner of the claret jug.

Young Tom had wanted to enter the Open in 1864, when he was only thirteen years old, but had been considered far too young to compete with the men. Three years later, he was allowed to compete in the oxymoronic Open Professional Tournament at Carnoustie, and he duly won the title. In that same year, 1867, he competed for the first time in the Open, and finished fourth out of ten competitors. His father was the winner that year. In 1868, aged seventeen years and five months, he won the Open for the first time, with a score of 157, five shots better than the previous record set by Andrew Strath when he won in 1865. He remains the youngest Open champion of all time. His scores in the next two years were even better: 154 and 149. He was bringing golf to new levels, and he was only nineteen years old.

Perhaps Young Tom would have become the W.G. Grace of golf; he was only three years younger, although far less bearded and rather more Scottish. He was certainly bringing his sport into the modern age as surely as W.G. was with cricket, and they both dominated their sport in a way that had not been seen before and would rarely be seen afterwards. However, the fates had other games to play with him. In September 1875, when he was twenty-four, he played a challenge match at North Berwick with his father against the brothers Willie and Mungo Park, both of whom had won the Open at least once. Willie Park was famous for the challenge matches he played for large stakes, and the Morrises were the toughest pair to play. On the final hole, Young Tom putted successfully for victory, but then was handed a telegram telling him that his wife was seriously ill after giving birth to their first child. They set out immediately for St Andrews, deciding to save time by taking a boat north to Anstruther across the Firth of Forth. But they were too late, and by the time they arrived home, both mother and baby were dead.

Young Tom never got over the loss, and lapsed into a deep melancholy. Two months later, he decided to accept a challenge from Captain Arthur Molesworth, a distinguished if eccentric amateur player from the Westward Ho! club in Devon, who was good enough to have won the Dowie Silver Cup at Hoylake in 1870. Molesworth had three clubs which he used almost to the exclusion of all others, and which he called "Faith", "Hope" and "Charity". "Faith" was his "play club", "Hope" was his iron, but as St Paul's epistle to the Corinthians teaches us, "the greatest of these is Charity", his putter. Unfortunately for Captain Molesworth, he was not very good at getting the ball in the air with any of these clubs, which helped earn him the nickname "The Mole". Molesworth, being an army officer, prided himself on his amateur status, but this did not prevent him from challenging professionals for money. In this instance, he challenged Young Tom to six rounds of golf, two a day for three days, with the Captain receiving six strokes a round.

It is hard to understand why Morris took the match; he was in no real state to play. His mind was not on his game, he was out of practice and he was thin and unfit, barely having eaten since his wife's death. To add to his difficulties, the weather was foul, with snow and ice across the Old Course at St Andrews. Nevertheless, Young Tom was far too good for Molesworth, who refused to give up until all hope of victory was gone. Morris won nine and seven, took the prize money and took to his bed, suffering from exhaustion, exposure, malnutrition and depression. Barely a month later, on Christmas Day 1875, he was found dead at home, aged just twenty-four. Old Tom never played in the Open again, but lived on until 1908, being eighty-seven years old when he died.

He spent his latter years concentrating on his club-making business. The advent of the guttie ball had created new demands on clubs, which now had to be stronger in the shaft and heavier in the head. Clubs which once survived many of the most incompetent players attacking the featheries were proving inadequate when even the greatest used the guttie. Among the most incompetent was Viscount Stormont. In the 1860s, when he was already over sixty years old, the portly Lord Stormont was told by his doctor to take up golf for the sake of his health. He was advised to go to Blackheath and put himself in the hands of Willie Dunn, the Scots golfer who was professional there until 1864. Stormont bought himself a set of brand new clubs, but after only five holes his caddie, Weever, reappeared at the professional's shop with an assorted collection of clubheads and shafts under his arm, and a request for a new set of clubs for his lordship. When Lord Stormont finally returned at the end of the round, Willie Dunn consoled him over the break-ages.

"Don't mention it," replied Stormont. "I feel already that this game has done me a great deal of good. I shall be down again on Thursday, and please have another set of clubs ready for me then."

The long-nosed wooden clubs with which Allan Robertson guided his featheries around St Andrews were neither strong enough nor shock-absorbent enough to deal with the guttie. Iron clubs rose to prominence almost overnight, and by the end of the century the leading manufacturers, such as Hugh Philp's nephew Robert Forgan, had created a new industry that was booming. The power of the new clubs and balls was well shown by the experiences of a golfer at Musselburgh in the 1860s who earned the nickname of "Kill The Cuddy", having hit a donkey, or cuddy, with his tee shot and killed it stone dead. We do not know for certain what the name of the golfer was, although there is plenty of circumstantial evidence to suppose that it was McGillicuddy, but we do know the maker of the club which drove the fatal ball. It was Robert Forgan.

It was not just the ordinary golf clubs and balls which sold well, either. As most players were entirely new to the game, they needed all the help they could get to keep their scores to within the calculating skills of the average adult. Thus we can read in the magazines of the day of Henley's "Melfort" Ball, which "has excellent flight, paint will not chip and it floats". The "Boodie" ball was also guaranteed to float, which may be why Weber patented the waterproof golf clubhead in 1899.

The speed at which golf grew in Britain and in the rest of the world in the latter part of the century was remarkable. Golf was essentially a middle-class participatory sport, like lawn tennis, but quite unlike association football, so the demand for courses on which to play was enormous, and the clamour for the chance to play on the courses that were already in existence was intense. In 1866, it was estimated there were about four thousand golfers worldwide, of whom over ninety-five per cent were in Britain, playing on the twenty-four courses then in existence. By 1876, there were almost eighty clubs in Britain, and by that time too, golf had spread to Australia, New Zealand, South Africa, Argentina and right across Europe. The number of players worldwide had probably quadrupled.

The responsibility for the rules of golf was only finally taken on by the R&A at St Andrews in 1897, when they formed their Rules of Golf Committee, although up to that date most clubs had followed the R&A rules more or less. All courses even today have their own particular rules to deal with the vagaries of the topography, but all follow the fundamental rules laid down by the R&A Rules of Golf Committee. By the end of the century, golf was firmly established on the sporting calendar, and was at that stage far more successful even than football and tennis in spreading overseas. The great and the good were still playing golf, of course, but so were the masses. Arthur Balfour, later to be prime minister and a man who, as we have seen, played a key role in the development of lawn tennis, was captain of the R&A in 1894, and all of Europe's royalty followed the example of King James VI and I and took up the game with enthusiasm.

They did not always excel at the game, nor even get the rules right. Queen Alexandra, the consort of Edward VII, tended to confuse the game with hockey, and once when playing with her daughter Princess Victoria and two courtiers, Sir Frederick Ponsonby and Sir Francis Knollys, on their private course at Sandringham, she seemed to be under the impression that the point of the game was to prevent your opponents from getting balls into the hole. As Sir Frederick later described it, "This usually ended by a scrimmage on the green. She also thought that the person who got into the hole first won it, and asked me to hurry up and run between strokes. It was very good fun and we all laughed."[2] Well, they would, wouldn't they? Sir Francis, incidentally, "always played in a square-shaped billycock hat and a London tail-coat, and hit so hard that his hat almost invariably fell off". So the tradition of wearing unsuitable clothing on the golf course was being maintained for future generations, so that people like Payne Stewart would have a well-connected precedent to point to.

It was not only royalty who took to golf with enthusiasm. The general public around the world was beginning to realise what a good way of getting exercise this ancient but nevertheless modern sport was, and from then on golf began its rapid climb to the levels of popularity it enjoys today.

"AN HONEST POT OF MONEY"

The Victorian era had witnessed the most astonishing growth of public sporting endeavours, thanks largely to the organising talents of a few noble-minded Englishmen (and one or two Scots) with more money and time than was reasonable, and who thus pursued leisure as an end in itself. What they did not realise, in their high-minded amateur way, was that they were laying the foundations of a major industry which would make multimillionaires of the descendants of the miners and cotton-mill workers for whom they were providing the means of escape from their daily drudgery and, eventually, their whole social class. This hugely professional business was created by a handful of amateurs.

By the end of the 19th century, only tennis and rugby union were still holding out against the pernicious grasp of professionalism. In golf, amateurs and professionals were allowed to play with and against each other, but only the professionals could take any prize money. Cricket managed a glorious middle path, a compromise so utterly British that it did not, of course, catch on anywhere else in the world. In all other countries, cricketers were just cricketers, but in Britain they remained either "Gentlemen" or "Players" until the 1960s.

Not that all the "Gentlemen" were strictly amateurs. Dr W.G. Grace, an amateur by classification but a professional in every other way, never received a wage for playing cricket, but he found ways of making money from the game. He followed the example of George Washington, who never received a salary as a General in the American War of Independence. He did, however, put in expense claims for such items as "food for one army", and the overall impression is of a man who did not go unrewarded for his efforts. Similarly, W.G. made sure that his efforts received their due rewards. In 1879, the year that W.G. finally qualified as a doctor at the age of thirty, there was also a national testimonial fund opened which raised enough to buy him a clock and two bronze ornaments and still have enough left over for a cheque for almost fifteen hundred pounds. In the winter of 1891–1892, he toured Australia as captain of the MCC team managed by Lord Sheffield, for which privilege he was paid three thousand pounds and all his expenses. This was broken-time payment gone mad, but of course his presence in England colours was worth far more to the tour organisers than a paltry three thousand pounds. After his astonishing season in 1895, when at the age of forty-seven he rewrote the record books yet again, there were no fewer than four funds opened for the good doctor; the Daily Telegraph's fund raised five thousand pounds, *The Sportsman* (where Charles Alcock worked) collected some more, the MCC committee added their little bit and Gloucestershire County Cricket Club created a fourth fund for its most prolific player. As Bernard Darwin wrote in his biography, "W.G. retired to his winter quarters the richer by an honest pot of money, £9,073 8s. 3d."[1] That's the way to be an amateur.

In tennis, there were professionals, whose role in life was to teach the rest of the world how to play the game; but because they were professionals, they were not allowed to compete in any of the world's major tournaments. So effectively, for the first century of the game's development, the leading tournaments were not won by the best players of the day, merely by the best players who had managed to persuade the authorities that they were not paid to play. When, in the 1950s and 1960s, Jack Kramer's professional tennis circuit attracted many of the leading amateurs to become full-time sportsmen, there was no doubt who were the best players. The likes of Pancho Gonzales, Ken Rosewall and Lew Hoad would have beaten any of their amateur rivals four times out of five. When Rod Laver turned pro in 1962, after winning Wimbledon twice in succession, he did not immediately assume the mantle of the greatest player in the world, but he didn't take too long. When Wimbledon was finally thrown open to the professionals in 1968, Laver came back and won the title that year and again in 1969. The professionals wiped the floor with the amateurs.

In soccer, the most thoroughly professional game of them all, there was still an amateur cup competition and the stirrings of amateur league competitions, but everyone agreed that most of the best players were professional. That did not prevent the occasional amateur from playing for England, but the days of distinguishing between the two classes on the pitch, as happened to James Forrest, the first professional to play for England, were over. The main backlash in football came from the Corinthians, a club founded by N.L. Jackson in 1882. Lane Jackson was chairman of the London Football Association, and had all his life been evangelical about the redeeming properties of sport and athletic pursuits among the lower classes. He sounds a real prig. He was also a journalist and editor of *Pastime*, a sports magazine. Despite the fact that he himself earned his living from sport, he was implacably opposed to professionalism and founded the Corinthians for public school and university men, to preserve all that was good about the amateur tradition. The club had no subscription fees; to allow the committee to keep out the wrong sort of fellow, it was limited to only fifty members and it owned no ground. Rule seven of the club stated categorically that "the Club shall not compete for any challenge cup or any prizes of any description whatever". This rule had to be amended in 1898 when the Sheriff of London Shield competition was endowed by Sir Thomas Dewar to raise money for local hospitals. The Shield was to be competed for by the best professional and amateur side of each year, and for reasons not unconnected with the fact that Lane Jackson was on the organising committee, the Corinthians entered – and usually won.

The Corinthians were one of the strongest sides in the country for perhaps two decades or more after their foundation. They were led on the field by Gilbert (G.O.) Smith, the Oxford University and England forward whose competition-free Corinthian ideals did not prevent him winning the amateur Cup with the Old Carthusians in 1897. In 1884, the Corinthians beat Blackburn Rovers, the Cup-holders, 8–1, and in 1904 they played Bury, who had just won the Cup by the biggest margin in history, beating Derby County 6–0. The Corinthians beat the Cup-holders by the amazing margin of 10–3. In those days they were a match for any other side in Britain.

Their amateur ideals were not necessarily as strictly adhered to as they would have had the world believe. A.N. "Monkey" Hornby, the Lancastrian cotton magnate who captained England at both cricket and rugby, and who was indeed a true amateur because he could afford to be, showed a remarkable lack of hypocrisy when he dived head first into the battle over rugby professionalism by telling the RFU that in his experience, the Corinthians asked for larger guarantees than professional clubs and paid expenses greater than the average professional club's wages bill.

Despite this apparently two-faced attitude to cash payments to its players, the Corinthians were indeed an amateur organisation. Their rules stipulated that they should not have a ground of their own and in many ways the ownership of real estate marks the difference between the professionals and the amateurs even more than the payments to players. Payment comes in many forms – a pay packet at the end of each week, a big money prize for winning a tournament, the proceeds from a testimonial or benefit match or even a few rolled up five pound notes stuffed into the boots of the so-called amateurs. But a ground is a ground is a ground. That is what turns a club into a business.

During the first years of organised team games in Britain, matches were played on common land, open parks or on grounds privately owned by major landlords. Matches were also played at schools and at cricket grounds owned or rented by the clubs involved, but it was not until the last decade of the 19th century that professional clubs began to build their own stadia on their own land. The need to accommodate the increasing numbers of spectators led to a new architectural sub-section, the architecture of sports grounds. In the quarter of a century between 1890 and the outbreak of the First World War, football and rugby stadia were built in every country of the world, and the skylines of many cities and towns were changed for ever. The leading light in all this was a man called Archibald Leitch, a Scottish engineer who built Hampden Park and Ibrox Park in

Glasgow, as well as Hillsborough, Stamford Bridge, Craven Cottage and Ayresome Park in England, to name but a few.

Leitch was first brought in to work with Rangers at Ibrox in 1900, when the three big Glasgow clubs were competing for the right to host the big football matches of each season, for which extra capacity was always needed. His West Stand open terracing opened in 1902 at a cost of twenty thousand pounds, but from the beginning there were doubts about its safety. Most Rangers fans soon learnt to avoid using the new West Stand terracing if possible, but when 68,114 people gathered there to watch Scotland v England on 5 April 1902, the first big match to come to Rangers largely because of their increased capacity, the West Stand was full. Six minutes after the kick-off, seven rows of the terracing's wooden planking collapsed under the weight of the spectators, and over one hundred spectators fell fifty feet to the ground through a hole thirty yards wide. Twenty-six of them were killed, but astonishingly the rest of the spectators in the ground were largely unaware of what was going on. The match was stopped briefly, but when first reports were that there were just a few injuries, the match was restarted. As one newspaper reported, "Not even the cries of dying sufferers nor the sight of broken limbs could attract this football maddened crowd from gazing upon their beloved sport." For the record, the game ended in a 1–1 draw but was later expunged from the official records; it was replayed in England in May, ending in a 2–2 draw.

Despite this setback, Leitch became the most important designer of football grounds of his time. He even carried on working with Rangers, expanding the ground capacity again in 1910 with earthen embankments at each end of the ground. On 1 January 1929, his career was crowned by the opening of what was then the grandest grandstand yet built in Britain – the ten thousand seat South Stand at Ibrox Park. The "maddened crowds" were being given ever greater opportunities for "gazing upon their beloved sport".

In 1896, the Corinthian ideal was deliberately spread around the world. The enigmatic and rather too earnest Baron Pierre de Coubertin created and staged the first modern Olympic Games. He had no stadium of his own – the Olympic movement, true to its amateur ideals, has never owned its own grounds – so they looked to other people to provide the geography while de Coubertin provided the philosophy. The idea of a modern Olympics was not particularly new: the title that W.G. Grace had won as a hurdler in 1866 was the National Olympian Sporting Association championship, so the Olympic name was in common enough use. It took a Frenchman, however, to build on the British Corinthian ideal and create what was for many years the final major bulwark of amateur international sport, before the late 20th century realities of national prestige and personal self-interest turned the games into yet another money-making jamboree.

Baron de Coubertin was a twenty-six-year-old French aristocrat when he was entrusted by the French government with the organisation of the Universal Exhibition in Paris in 1889, for which the Eiffel Tower was built. This experience gave him the enthusiasm and the experience, not to mention the contacts, to attempt to organise an international athletics meeting which he called the Olympic Games. As he said, "The name imposed itself: it was not even possible to find another."

De Coubertin's motivation was that of the pure amateur. In his introductory speech at the Games, he noted that "there was a commercial spirit which threatened to invade sporting circles.

Wherever they ran or wrestled openly for money, one nonetheless senses the tendency to regrettable compromises, and in the urge for victory something quite other than ambition and sense of honour came into play. With the risk of seeing athletics degenerate and die for a second time, it became necessary to unify it and purify it."

In his view, there was "but one method to achieve this: to create competitions at regular intervals at which representatives of all countries and all sports would be invited under the aegis of the same authority, which would impart to them a halo of grandeur and glory". No money, just a halo of grandeur and glory. That's what the Olympics should be about.

De Coubertin was entirely aware of how sport had come to occupy such a central place in the minds of the leaders of Europe.

"There are many points," he said, "upon which criticism might be brought against the education which takes place in English public schools; yet it is beyond any contradiction that the education in them is both strong and virile. One can attribute, to a large extent, the expansion and strength of the British Nation, to which the English have been elevated during the reign of Queen Victoria, to the virtues of this upbringing." He noted the difference between the English and the French education systems; in Britain, there was value placed on "the contribution of the muscles to the work of moral education. In France on the contrary, until recently, physical inertia was considered the necessary corollary to mental development."

Despite Baron de Coubertin's well-known love of Britain, he found great difficulty in getting the British to agree to take part in his Olympics. Given the arguments that very quickly developed internally within British sporting institutions, it is hardly surprising that they found it difficult to agree with any outsiders. The National Cyclists Union, for example, resisted for a long time, and the Amateur Rowing Association was even more difficult. In the end, there was no rowing event in the first Olympic Games, for reasons of bad weather rather than in revenge for the barriers put up against de Coubertin's attempts to help French rowers race at Henley. That had taken ten months of negotiations, as well as the intervention of the French Ambassador in London, before finally they were allowed to take part.

Persistence ran deep in the veins of the Baron, however, and he never gave up. A meeting was called for the Great Hall of the University of the Sorbonne in Paris in June 1894, at which de Coubertin planned to propose holding a first Olympic Games in 1900. The enthusiasm of the delegates, however, was unstoppable. They voted for a first Olympics to take place in Athens in 1896, and on 6 April that year, Easter Monday, with fifty-nine athletes from ten nations gathered for the inauguration ceremony performed by the King of the Hellenes, the first modern Olympic Games opened. The events included were for the most part familiar to modern eyes, but in some cases distinctly odd. The athletics contests included the 100 metres, 400 metres, 800 metres and 1500 metres, as well as high jump, long jump and the marathon, a race specially invented for the occasion and which was won by the Greek hero of the games, an eighteen-year-old shepherd called Spiridon Louis. Nine of the fifteen athletics contests produced gold medals for the Americans (actually silver medals, which were awarded to the winners that year, with bronze medals to the runner-up and nothing for the third-place finisher), but England picked up the winner's medal for "Lifting the Weight with One Hand", an abstruse art perfected by one L. Elliott, who had also competed in the 100 metres.

The next two Olympic Games, in 1900 and 1904, were such a shambles that it was surprising that the Olympic movement survived. The 1900 games, held in Paris, were only designated Olympic Games at the very last moment, more as a favour to de Coubertin than anything else – they had originally been planned as part of another international exposition in Paris that year – but all the same there were over double the number of athletes competing, this time from a total of sixteen countries. As a result, not everybody knew they had been competing in an Olympic Games, and the fact that the winner's medal for cricket was won by England is a curiosity that remained remarkably hidden from public knowledge for about eighty years. The 1904 games were held in St Louis, spread over a period of four and a half months almost as a sideshow to the Louisiana Purchase Exposition, commemorating the date when France sold Louisiana to the United States for three million dollars, a hundred and one years earlier in 1803. The Games were so low key that de Coubertin did not even bother to go, and Tom Kiely, a thirty-five-year-old Irishman who won the "All Around Championship" (an early version of the decathlon), had to pay his own fare, and was not acknowledged as an Olympic champion until fifty years later.

The events which were included or excluded in each Olympics were the subjects of decisions which at times appeared arbitrary, but the main athletics and swimming events have always survived. The marathon, the one event which has over the years come to symbolise the Games, almost fell by the wayside before the 1924 Games in Paris. It was proposed, and accepted, at a meeting of the International Olympic Congress in 1921, that the marathon should be dropped and in its place a prize should be awarded for "the most outstanding event in mountain climbing". It proved hard to stage this event in Paris, where even the most unobservant would notice the lack of suitable mountain ranges, so they reversed the decision and went back to the marathon, which was duly won by Albin Stenroos of Finland.

The Olympic Games were a triumph of the amateur ideals, and more than other single-sports events, they kept the ultimate victory of professionalism at bay. In other areas of British life, the social and political influence of the Corinthian classes, to whom all money was vulgar and new money positively unspeakable, was almost over. When Keir Hardie was elected as Labour MP for West Ham in 1892, he arrived at Westminster accompanied by a brass band. The domination of British institutions and the upper echelons of the British social hierarchy by the landed gentry and the industrialists was about to come to an end – not with a bang but with a long drawn out whimper. The role of government in all aspects of British life was about to increase dramatically, and sport would not escape the watchful eye of Westminster.

The power of the administrators has largely been usurped by the power of the sponsors and the power of the media, but these developments are not new. Commercial organisations, who see a marketing advantage in being associated with a sporting success, have existed since the earliest days of organised sport. Companies like Spiers and Pond, the catering firm who underwrote the cost of the early English cricket tours, or Lipton's Tea who were involved with early America's Cup yacht races are the direct spiritual ancestors of Benson and Hedges, Barclays Bank and Canon who have all been closely involved with sports sponsorship in more recent times. Professional sport soon recognised that it could not survive purely on spectators' gate money alone, so even in Victorian times, sponsorship deals were being put together, for the equal benefit of player, spectator and, of course, sponsor. In all sports, there was a rapid increase in the number of spectators who came to the events, culminating in the hundred and twenty-five thousand or so who came to Wembley to see Bolton Wanderers play West Ham United in the 1923 Cup final, the first staged at the new Imperial Stadium. Cricket, tennis, rugby, golf and a host of other sports enjoyed huge gates between the wars and in the immediate post-war years, when there was an increasing amount of free time for people to spend watching their heroes and heroines play, but not yet enough free time to take long and expensive overseas holidays, one of the many different options which compete these days for the leisure dollars of the world. But even so, when there was a captive audience and a severe limit on the amount of money that even the greatest sportsmen could earn, gate money was not enough. The sponsors had a vital role to play.

As the old millennium gives way to the new, television, radio and newspaper companies who report the sports, increasingly seem to be trying to gain exclusive access to events which they can then make their own. Thus we may get upset when a particular sports event is only to be seen on a subscriber TV channel, or when a particular newspaper devotes much of its sporting column inches to an event to which it has secured the rights. The danger is that this will result in the sportsmen and women (and dogs and horses, camels and pigeons) having to adapt their sport to the needs of the medium that tells their story to the world. We fear that the real spectator, the true lover of the sport, is being upstaged by those at one remove. We must defend our right to have a say in our favourite sports, even if, when push comes to shove, we are far more likely to watch them on television or read about them in the papers than to bother to go along to the grounds to witness them at first hand. We are all spectators at one remove, but we like to think we are real ones.

There is nothing new in this. In the 19th century, newspapers were just as keen to gain exclusive coverage of sports events as they are today, perhaps even more so, but looking back over a period of one hundred years, it no longer seems so significant. After all, who is interested in yesterday's news? Yet at the time, there were many newspapers which tried to gain exclusive rights to all sorts of events which we would feel ought to be in the public domain – whatever that means – rather than the exclusive property of one news medium. The newspaper tycoons of the 19th century soon learnt that sports events, being part news stories and part theatrical occasions, are particularly easy to control and can yield spectacular returns.

But only for a very short time. Once any match is over, it is in the public domain and has no further value, so the battles to be the first to bring the news to the public are quickly forgotten. The aerial battles that took place over Wembley Stadium when the Cup final was played there on 25 April 1936 have been long forgotten, but the result remains easily accessible. Arsenal beat Sheffield United by a Ted Drake goal in the seventy-fifth minute to nil, but the real story of the day was the dispute between the Wembley Stadium authorities and the newsreel companies over the rights to the match. As a result, Wembley refused to allow any of the newsreel cameramen into the ground to film the game. So the news cameramen did what any enterprising journalist would have done and hired light aeroplanes and autogyros to fly or hover over the stadium to film the action from the air. Unluckily for them, the Wembley management got wind of their plans and brought in search-lights for the day, which they shone directly at the aircraft to prevent any clear photos or films from being taken. This caused a sensation at the time, but not, fortunately, any mid-air colli-sions; the coverage would have been good if there had been. Sixty years on, the airborne events of that day are a mere foot-note at best in any history of sport or the media. It does not really matter whether there is any action film of the 1936 Cup final available to us now, taken from the air, from the touchline or from the Royal Box by King Edward himself, because we know the score and can read the newspaper reports. It will be the same in sixty years from now, when people will not care which media mogul secured the rights to the Grand National or the World Cup or the Olympic Games because the whole thing will be freely available on whatever the viable technology of the day might be. The life expectancy of a profitable sporting story is very short.

Fans who actually want to play sports represent a further wonderful opportunity for money-making. They always have. The kit required to play any sport these days may appear to be getting more and more sophisticated and thus more and more expensive, but it was ever thus. We have already seen how much golf clubs and balls cost in the mid-1800s, and cricket bats were no cheaper – except of course that most people only needed one bat per game. In 1773, cricket bats were advertised for sale at four shillings, a price which had risen a hundred years later to ten shillings, when J. Browning of Bristol patented the triangu-lar cross-section bat, a shape that still dominates today. By this time, the best bats were made of willow, with handles of cane with rubber strips inserted to give extra whip to the bat when the ball was struck. By late Victorian times there were perhaps twenty cricket-bat manufacturers in London alone, such was the demand. For every cricket bat bought, there would also have to be pads, batting gloves and balls, not to mention stumps, flannels and caps. The market in multi-coloured caps distinguishing every cricket club flourished between 1850 and 1950, with some players preferring to wear an Incogniti or I Zingari cap even when playing for county or country.

Nowadays, even the feeblest competitors want to look the part, so we can see hundreds of Pete Sampras or Martina Hingis clones on the tennis courts, with the latest rackets and the most prestigious name on the shirts, trying desperately to get the ball back over the net at least once every half hour or so. We see batsmen kitted out like Brian Lara striding to the wicket on a thousand village greens every Saturday or Sunday afternoon, and we see those same Laras trudging disconsolately back to the pavilion one or two balls later. There are thousands of golfers all wearing Nick Faldo shirts or Greg Norman hats and using their Arnold Palmer drivers to slice their latest aerodynamically sound balls into the lake or the bunker or at least as far as the ladies' tees. There are even cyclists who can barely get their bikes going faster than walking speed who are proud possessors of the complete Chris Boardman figure-hugging Tour de France shirts and shorts, not to mention those wind-assisted helmets which make even the greatest sportsmen look complete idiots. If you want to climb a little hill these days, you have to look like Chris Bonington preparing to bivouac on the north face of the Eiger, and even the joggers look set for a double marathon every time they potter out where others can see them. Thank goodness for darts.

Sport has become fashionable, and sports equipment is a part of the fashion industry. This was never the case in the early years of organised sport, and it was probably not until Suzanne Lenglen showed her style and her legs on the tennis court in the 1920s that sport and fashion began to move a little closer together. It had taken some time for women tennis players to break free from the tight dresses and boaters which Lottie Dod and Maud Watson had been condemned to wear, but once they loosened up, there was no stopping them. Elizabeth "Bunny" Ryan, the American tennis champion of the 1920s, said, "All women tennis players should go down on their knees in thankfulness to Suzanne Lenglen for delivering them from the tyranny of corsets." They overtook the men in the freedom of their outfits – the men were still wearing long flannels until past the Second World War. Teddy Tinling and René Lacoste, himself a tennis champion, between them turned tennis into a fashionable experience with their fashions which made the most of as little white cotton as they could get away with to cover the bodies of the players and the sensibilities of the centre court spectators. Lacoste's little alligator was the badge to be seen wearing, and Tinling's frilly knickers caused a sensation when "Gorgeous" Gussie Moran of the United States first wore them at Wimbledon in the 1950s.

Money now surrounds sport from all sides, so who can blame the best players when they try to prolong their high-earning seasons? W.G. Grace played for England into his fifties and Old Tom Morris was unbeatable at golf at the same age, so the stars of today are only following in a well-established tradition. The rise of "seniors" tournaments in golf, tennis and even cricket is the perfect answer to what to do with the sportsman or woman who cannot face the idea of "retirement" at an age when the rest of us are just getting into our working stride. Julius Boros the golfer was once asked if he had any plans to retire, and he replied, "Why should I retire? All I do now is play golf and go fishing." If enough people to fill Wembley Stadium will pay to watch the Rolling Stones play in their fifties, why shouldn't Jack Nicklaus and Viv Richards have the chance to sell a few tickets to people who want to savour a glimpse of the skills they used to have? The Victorians never expected this to happen, because they did not consider that the sports they were involved with were there for the spectators; they thought they were there for the players. But there are always more spectators than players (except at a county cricket ground on a wet Thursday morning in May), so the spectators, whether on the spot or at one remove, are the people the clever marketers target.

The Victorians who created our sporting world – men like Charles Alcock, Walter Wingfield, the Earl of Eglinton, Charles Thring and even William Webb Ellis – were idealists but also entrepreneurs. They may have been trying, in the spirit of the times, to improve the lot of the common man but at the same time they were anything but revolutionaries. They were all men whose position in society was not in doubt and who had no desire to change the social order or their position in it. They were of the ruling class and they intended to stay there. But what they actually created was one of the biggest forces for social change in the 20th century. When soccer spread like wildfire around the globe, it brought with it an equality of opportunity and of status which many players had never experienced in their lives until they were on the soccer pitch. This was heady stuff, and was not to be thrown away lightly. When the English spread the gospel of cricket across the Empire, they were distributing a weapon which would rebound on them, a weapon with which the colonials could beat the Imperial masters. Even today, England is the country most teams like to beat, even though it is often not a particularly hard feat to accomplish.

Sport is the great equaliser, a huge liberating force all around the world. The equality of sport is not to do with birth, with education or with money. It is simply to do with athletic ability. This is a hugely subversive idea, that the leaders of a major section of society (and the heroes of even more people) cannot be selected at birth. Their talents can of course be nurtured from a young age, as has happened in vastly different circumstances with, for example, East German swimmers or Tiger Woods, but sporting heroes achieve their status on their own terms; and there is no way of controlling how long they will retain that position. Sporting heroes are not like presidents, elected for four or five or seven years. They are there as long as they can be, or as long as they want to be. Their status is beyond outside control, even more so than the fickle popularity of a Rudolf Valentino or the Spice Girls, for example. Sporting success is not like a film or pop star's popularity. It does not come and go in quite the same sudden way, because sporting success is measured far more objectively and does not always go hand-in-hand with public acclaim, as many sportsmen and women, from Paul Gascoigne and Geoffrey Boycott to O.J. Simpson and Harold Larwood, have discovered. No wonder the societies which most pride themselves on equality, but equality on their own terms, are the ones that have tried most carefully to control sport.

Those societies, for example those of communist East Europe before the collapse of the Berlin Wall, were only doing what the Victorians were trying to do. They were trying to impose their will and their rules on something which really belonged to everybody. When Charles Thring drafted his rules for "The Simplest Game", he was trying to impose order on football for the good of the people who played it. Stalin's apologists may well have argued that in the Soviet Union he was merely imposing order on his country for the good of the people who lived there. It is unfair to compare a mid-Victorian sporting schoolmaster who probably did nothing more violent than cane a dozen boys in his time, with a Russian dictator with the blood of millions on his hands, but the idea of control is common to both. The Victorian administrators, as self-elected as any Stalin or Mao or Castro, were trying to establish a means of control over the sports they loved, and they would have justified their actions by saying it was for the good of the people. The communist dictators told the world they were revolutionaries, but were really intent only on reinforcing and conserving their own positions. Charles Alcock, Pierre de Coubertin et al, on the other hand, were revolutionaries without meaning to be. They thought they were merely reinforcing the status quo, but their efforts ended up playing a significant part in the collapse of the 19th century social hierarchy.

They created a whole new world of leisure activity, a multi-billion dollar world-wide industry, a source of hopes and dreams, a cause of wars, revolutions and social upheavals – and they thought they were just making up a few rules and organising a few competitions so that a handful of fit young men could have fun.

Notes

Chapter 1
[1] *Oxford Companion to Sports and Games*, Oxford University Press, 1976
[2] Barbara W. Tuchman, *A Distant Mirror*, Macmillan, 1978
[3] Quoted by Tony Money, *Manly and Muscular Diversions*, Duckworth, 1997
[4] Pierce Egan, *Boxiana*, 1824
[5] Robert Burton, *The Anatomy of Melancholy*, 1621
[6] *Harmsworth's Encyclopaedia*, 1922

Chapter 2
[1] G.M. Trevelyan, *English Social History*, Longmans 1942
[2] Vivian Ogilvie, *The English Public School*, Batsford, 1957
[3] *Harmsworth's Encyclopaedia*, 1922
[4] R.L. Archer, *Secondary Education in the Nineteenth Century*, London, 1921
[5] Peter Wynne-Thomas, *The History of Cricket*, HMSO, 1997
[6] H.E.M. Icely, *Bromsgrove School Through Four Centuries*, Blackwell, 1953
[7] D.O. and P.W. Neely, *The Summer Game*, Moa Beckett, New Zealand, 1994
[8] G.M. Trevelyan, *English Social History*, Manchester University Press, 1942
[9] Derek Birley, *Sport and the Making of Britain*, 1993

Chapter 3
[1] Rowland Bowen, *Cricket: A History of its Growth and Development*, Eyre & Spottiswoode, 1970
[2] H.S. Altham, *A History of Cricket*, Volume 1, George Allen and Unwin, 1926
[3] W.G. Grace, *W.G. Cricketing Reminiscences and Personal Recollections*, J. Bowden, 1899
[4] A.L. Ford, *Curiosities of Cricket*, D.B. Friend & Co., 1895

Chapter 4
[1] *The Story of the Football League*, Football League Ltd, 1938
[2] *The Story of the Football League*, Football League Ltd, 1938
[3] J.F. Ramsay, *The Growth of Association Football*, London, 1895

Chapter 5
[1] Charles Alcock, *Football on The Oval*, London 1904

Chapter 6
[1] Derek Birley, *Sport and the Making of Britain*, Manchester University Press, 1993
[2] *Windsor Magazine*, August 1895
[3] *Wisden Cricketers' Almanack*, 1878 edition
[4] *Wisden Cricketers' Almanack*, 1874 edition
[5] *Windsor Magazine*, August 1895

Chapter 7
[1] Robert Clark, *Golf: a Royal and Ancient Game*, Edinburgh 1899
[2] Sir Frederick Ponsonby, *Recollections of Three Reigns*, Eyre and Spottiswoode, 1951

Chapter 8
[1] Bernard Darwin, *W.G. Grace*, Duckworth, 1934

INDEX